A. R. Western

Hyde Park Sketches

A. R. Western

Hyde Park Sketches

ISBN/EAN: 9783337826604

Printed in Europe, USA, Canada, Australia, Japan

Cover: Foto ©Andreas Hilbeck / pixelio.de

More available books at **www.hansebooks.com**

HYDE PARK SKETCHES.

BY

A. R. WESTERN.

"Hyde Park Sketches" will be welcomed by two classes of society; namely, by "stay-at-home travellers," and by those, less numerous, who visit the old country (as it is often called), and instead of being lost, as it were, in the immense and absorbing population of London, apply themselves to the cultivation of an intimate acquaintance with its localities and their traditions, with the inhabitants and their oft-times singular habits, customs, and eccentricities. The author has taken Hyde Park as the centre of what may be called metropolitan in contradistinction to commercial London. He used his eyes to observe, his ears to listen, his voice to inquire, his memory to retain, and his pen to record all that he had learned about the highways and bye-ways of the greatest city on earth. Original characters are described with vivid force, eccentric persons are brought forward, and the veins of fact and fiction run commingled through the pages. Nothing dull appears in these sketches, in which "the West End" of mighty London is made to pass before us, as in review. Tradition and history are blended, and a severe critic, who examined the work carefully, has expressed his admiration of the manner in which historic truth has been preserved inviolate all through. It may be safely predicted that Londoners themselves, on reading this volume, will be surprised to learn how little they actually know of their own city, and how well the author is acquainted with it.

PHILADELPHIA:
T. B. PETERSON & BROTHERS;
306 CHESTNUT STREET.

PREFACE.

The title of these sketches was adopted by me, because Hyde Park was the best place for seeing a variety of people; and they were hastily written, as one friend would write to another.

I have not submitted the MS. to the inspection of any one, and I am not sure of the favorable reception of the book; but I can only express the hope that it will be kindly received.

THE AUTHOR.

Paris, December 6th, 1879.

CONTENTS.

		Page
I.	THE GENTLEMAN IN BLACK	23
II.	STREET PREACHING IN LONDON	26
III.	A PARK OWNER	29
IV.	IN ROTTEN ROW	32
V.	OUT OF DOOR ECCENTRICS	38
VI.	THEATRICALS EXTRAORDINARY	43
VII.	A MUSEUM VISITOR	47
VIII.	THE DESERTED ROOM	53
IX.	SWELLS AND CANINES	61
X.	FRENCH PEOPLE	64
XI.	THE ENGLISH	68
XII.	A BATCH OF ARTISANS	74
XIII.	BENHAFIT AND A BEAR STORY	78
XIV.	ENGLAND AND AMERICA	84
XV.	CO-OPERATIVE STORES	90
XVI.	BENHAFIT IN THE PARK	93
XVII.	THE GENERAL'S FEATS	100

CONTENTS.

		Page
XVIII.	SELF-MADE MEN	107
XIX.	A TROUBLED LIFE	111
XX.	PLACES AND PEOPLE	125
XXI.	THE DRAPER'S STORY	132
XXII.	HOW AN M. P. GETS ON	147
XXIII.	GENTLEMEN OF THE BAR	154
XXIV.	VICISSITUDES OF FASHION	159
XXV.	JOHN CUFF AND THE SEAL	162
XXVI.	THE CONFIDENTIAL CLERK	171
XXVII.	THE CHEVALIER ST. GEORGE	187
XXVIII.	HYDE PARK IN SEVERAL REIGNS	199
XXIX.	VARIETIES OF POPULAR AMUSEMENTS	208

HYDE PARK SKETCHES.

I.

THE GENTLEMAN IN BLACK.

HYDE PARK is pleasantly situated in what may be called the best part of London, and contains about four hundred acres of fine ground, with trees and shrubs, and for the summer are planted a large and rare collection of beautiful flowers. There are roads for carriages and vehicles of every description; also roads for equestrians, and firm walks for pedestrians.

As may be supposed, this place is a popular resort for people of all ranks, and among the number are a few singular persons, who are usually designated as absent-minded. Their minds are absent, and so far distant, that with the swiftest of horses they could never reach them in this sphere, and it may be hoped that they will hereafter be more successful.

Among the number of these persons is a gentleman of the medium size and height, who is said to be seventy years of age, whose hair and whiskers, (both being kept in the best order,) are black as night, and he evidently is rather proud of them. He dresses entirely in black, and at all seasons of the year wears a long cloak, tight-fitting trowsers, and very high top boots, with a hat of the usual quality worn by gentlemen, but twice as high as the present style, and of a sugar-loaf shape. His neck is much longer than the neck of the most of other persons, and is always encased with a black velvet stock reaching to his ears, and causing him to carry his head very high.

He also wears black kid gloves, reaching up nearly half of the way to his elbows, and ever has an umbrella — nearly twice the size of that of any other person, in or out of the park — which he carries under his arm, always in the same way.

This gentleman never speaks or takes the least notice of any one. He stalks (among the throng who are walking and sitting in the chairs) with a slow, measured step; occasionally stopping, and turning around, first one way and then the other, (as he finds it difficult to turn his head,) with a pleased expression of countenance, as if he was perfectly satisfied with every thing that he saw, and did not wish to make any change.

After he has been in the Park for about two hours, he departs, and is seen no more for the day. He does not visit Hyde Park *every* day; probably he is seen there twice a week, and he evidently visits the other Parks, which are numerous in London.

The weather is sometimes quite warm in the summer in England, and the reverse in winter; but this gentleman always appears in the same clothes, which — like his hair and whiskers — are in the very best condition.

He is said to be in good circumstances, in a pecuniary way; but has worn a remarkable dress, and has had strange ideas and manners, for the greater part of his life.

He has good rooms in a good boarding establishment; partakes of his meals in his room, and never speaks to any one, in the house, or out of the house, if he can possibly avoid doing so.

II.

STREET PREACHING IN LONDON.

NEAR the Regents Park, one afternoon, I heard a street preacher, who had a large but promiscuous audience. He was a young man of fine appearance, well dressed, with a good address, and was heard with attention through his discourse, which lasted nearly twenty-five minutes.

When he had concluded, another person filled the vacated place, and said that every thing the other man had said was wrong; but before he proceeded to prove that such was the fact, he wished to say that "he had the highest possible regard for the person who had just finished, and for the audience. Many of them were full of superstition," he said, "but he would eradicate all of that in a mighty short time."

He was rather an unwholesome-looking individual, with a dingy suit of black; the coat buttoned up to the neck, with not a vestige of a shirt collar. He was walking on the sides of his shoes, and his trowsers were short, which caused a display of stockings in a doubtful state. His hat was tall, and matched his other apparel, and that hat contained a large handkerchief of many colors.

His hair was thick, black and bushy, and his face of a peculiar color — which is owned by those classes who are sometimes partial to the open air at night.

He continued his discourse by saying that he doubted the ancients ever saying what they were reported to have said; but if they did ever say so, they were wrong; and then he went on for some time, endeavoring to prove something — but what that something was I could not tell. But he continued saying, that he never believed any thing unless he saw it — he never believed he had any money unless he had it in his hand or in his pocket; and he gave his pocket a slap to make the coin jingle, but hearing no noise of that kind, he straightened himself and threw his head back and endeavored to prove the existence of a shirt collar, but after working away for several moments, and not being able to find it, he gave it up as a "lost cause," and used his handkerchief over his hair and face.

He proceeded to say that all mankind had their origin from the lowest forms of animated nature, and grew like weeds; and he looked about him as if he expected to see several weeds, but seeing nothing so weedy as himself, his look became more circumscribed.

He said that the world was perfectly flat — the edges might be a little round, but the top was flat, and he believed the bottom was flat also; for he had looked into the matter well, and he *knew* that such was the fact.

In continuation, he announced the world was disappearing very fast, and, in a few years, or in a comparatively few years — say in two or three hundred thousand — would all be washed away; and, if not washed away, it would be destroyed by earthquakes or volcanoes, which would amount to the same thing. He now in a metaphorical sense, got into deep water and floundered a little; but soon emerged, when he said that what he stated was as true as that he would have a lodging and bed that night.

The audience now were skeptical, and he was desired to let some other speaker take his place.

III.

A PARK OWNER.

A YOUNG man about thirty or thirty-five years of age, who is always well dressed, visits the Park nearly every day, and walks on nearly every road, going rapidly, and only speaking to the workmen (who are always doing something, or pretending to do something, about the place,) and to the policemen. But I am mistaken — for he does speak to the bare-headed, bare-footed little street Arabs, and sometimes he runs after them, as if he would drive them from the Park, when they climb the trees, and hang on to the railings or occupy the chairs.

All these little vagabonds know him pretty well, and pay but little attention to him. He is in reality harmless, but those who have seen him for the first time, might think differently.

This young man believes himself to be the owner of the Park, and thinks that the policemen and workmen who are there are his servants, and although he permits persons to visit the place who behave themselves, imagines that he alone has the right, and the power to enforce that right, which consists in ordering carriages, equestrians and pedestrians to leave immediately, and not to come there any more. He declared his intention, at one time, (to the policemen) of shutting the gates and keeping them locked, for he remarked that some people would walk on the grass, and others climb the trees, and although they did not injure his property, he was annoyed by them, so, to keep them out of his grounds, he feared that he should be compelled to close the gates; and exclude every one, even those who were well behaved. He said that he would regret to be compelled to take this course, because there were some very deserving people who visited his estate; but if a portion of the persons who came to *his* Park were unruly, he could not separate them from the better class, so to protect his trees, shrubs, flowers and grass, he feared that he should have to close his gates against all.

The policemen finally told him that the power of the Government was supreme, and desired the gates to be opened to the people; and if his property was damaged, the Government would pay for the damage. This pacified him for the time, but he looks at the vast throng sometimes, as if he thought they were taking great liberties. He never speaks to any of the visitors who ride or drive, or to any of the gentlemen who walk, for, as he thinks that he owns the finest estate in London, he considers himself above all others in that vast city.

He will talk about the improvements he intends making, in a year or two. He thinks that he shall have the Serpentine river, (which is an elongated pond,) enlarged, and that he will construct a fine cascade or waterfall, either at one or the other end of the lake.

He says that he will purchase some American Bisons, and have them turned loose in the largest part of his vacant grounds, as these animals might keep some of the people off of the grass.

This person has wealthy friends who take good care of him; but some one has evidently made him believe that he is the owner of the Park, and he does believe it firmly.

Whether he will appoint a successor when he retires, remains to be seen.

IV.

IN ROTTEN ROW.

THERE is undoubtedly a great deal of pleasure in riding on a very good horse in Rotten Row in the parliamentary season. In the first place the road is about the best in the world, as there has been no expense spared to make it perfect. It is a little over one mile in length, and about one hundred feet wide. The horses seem to enjoy traveling on the magnificent road, just as their riders seem to enjoy it with them. There is no part of England or Europe, where the people at large appear to enjoy themselves so well as they do in this place; nor is there any part of Europe, where the ladies ride so well, or look better, than they do in the two mile road, called Rotten Row, in Hyde Park.

A gentleman in London, giving his experience in riding, or in attempting to ride, in Rotten Row, told the tale of his adventure in the following manner:

He went to a stable, to which he had been recommended, and informed one of the young men (or *boys*, as they are sometimes called in the stables,) that he wanted a good saddle horse to ride in the Park. While I think of it, I will state that this gentleman is about thirty-seven years old, about five feet ten in height, and a little inclined to be stout. He is universally good natured, and universally popular.

The stable "boy" looked at him for a moment, and said, "I thinks as how you might ride a good horse much betterer than some other gentlemen mightened ride a worserer hanimal." My friend had heard the letter H badly insulted, but had never before heard the Queen's English insulted in this way. He said in reply to the "boy" that he was sure of it—he had not thought of it before, but since it was mentioned, he knew that he was quite correct.

He could not for the life of himself make out what the "boy" was trying to get at. But he continued, "oh yes," "certainly," "quite so," "yes indeed," "quite true."

The "boy" looked very much pleased, and showed him to a door through which a horse was visible. But, as he came near, the animal gave a squeal, making a noise similar to the noises made by horses when they bite each other, and simultaneously with the squeal, threw up his hind foot in such a way, that if the proposed rider had been eight inches further to the right, his head would have been in some considerable jeopardy.

"What did he do that for?" asked the aspirant for Rotten Row. "Well, master," said the young reformed grammarian, "you sees as how he has white hind legs, and I actually thinks, as he believes he wears white trousers, and you observes that his legs are werry nice." "But," said the impatient equestrian, "what made him squeal in that disagreeable way? I always thought horses squealed when they were angry, or were biting each other."

The "boy," watchful of his master's interests, answered, "It has allers struck me, that when that horse squeals, he means to laugh, for you knows dogs barks when they plays, and they barks when they bites."

By this time the horse was saddled and bridled, and looked all ready for the road. As he was led out in front of the stable, with his head towards the Park, the gentleman saw that all of the employés of the stables, were apparently very much pleased and interested about something; for they were laughing all of the time. He liked to see persons good-natured. Upon his word and honor, it was quite refreshing. He saw now that he had forgotten his spurs. So he asked for a pair. When he made this request the young men's mirth appeared to increase. He thought it was very remarkable that people should laugh because he asked for a pair of spurs. Almost everybody wore spurs, in Rotten Row.

At length, one of the young men came forward, and said, "I think, sir, that you will do better without spurs, as the horse is sometimes a trifle ticklish."

One man stood on one side of the animal, holding one rein, and another stood directly on the other side, holding the other, while the "boy" helped the gentleman into the saddle.

The first thing the horse did, when the top of the saddle was reached, was to stand upon his hind legs. Then he changed and stood on his fore legs; and next he endeavored to elevate all of his feet at one time; but, not being able to do this, suddenly elevated his back, like the back of a camel, and at about the same time stood on his fore legs.

Our friend now *withdrew from the horse*, and proceeded in front, about twenty feet in the direction of the Park.

He had been a little unfortunate in withdrawing from the horse, for he had fallen, and in doing so he had nearly separated one leg of his trowsers from the remaining portion; his hat was damaged, and he had left behind one of the skirts of his coat, which was hanging to the saddle. He had also found the road quite dusty.

He went to the proprietor of the horse, and told him that he had concluded *not* to ride in Rotten Row that day, but when he did resolve to do so, would inform him a day or two before, if he should wish to ride one of *his* horses. So that the animal could be all ready for him when he arrived at the stable.

He frankly admits that he has never regretted the absence of the spurs.

* * * * * *

There is a gentleman whose age is quite uncertain, but he is known to the oldest visitor of Hyde Park. He is a fine looking man; his clothes are of the best quality, and of the most approved style. About five years ago his hair and whiskers were black as black can be. He disappeared for a few months, and people were afraid that this patriarch had left the Park of life.

When he reappeared, his hair and whiskers were perfectly white.

No one knows how old he is, but some say that he was old when Tyburn tree was abolished, which was over sixty years ago. If he was old at that time, he must be now over one hundred and twenty years of age. But people are sometimes mistaken in regard to ages.

When this gentleman walks in the Park he gets into the very thickest part of the crowd, and if there are comparatively *few* to notice him, then he goes in a path where there are *no* persons.

It is either one thing or the other with him, and no half-way work. In one respect he is like all semi-lunatics, and will not speak to any one if he can avoid doing so.

He is wealthy, very kind and charitable, almost to a fault — if that can be.

V.

OUT OF DOOR ECCENTRICS.

WHEN there are large numbers occupying the seats by the paths in Rotten Row, a gentleman of middle age, and dressed in the usual mode, with a single eye-glass of unusual size, walks by the lines of ladies and gentlemen, and removing his hat — bows in the most approved fashion; and, smiling as he does so, sometimes remarks on the fine weather, and other interesting topics. After he has gone through the lines and reviewed them completely he departs. His friends keep him at home, as much as possible; but he will sometimes get away from them,— and then goes directly to Hyde Park; remaining there for one or two hours. He makes his appearance irregularly, by sometimes once in a week, or once in a fortnight.

Another middle-aged gentleman is occasionally seen in the most frequented parts of Hyde Park, who attracts more attention than any of the remarkable persons.

He is a little under the medium size; and is the most perfect combination of the gentleman and the vagabond that can be possibly imagined. His walk and manners are like those of the most finished gentleman in London or Paris; but it would be difficult to find in either place a more partially ragged individual.

His coat, or coats, for he wears two; — the under one being buttoned, and the outside one not, so as to display the inside coat,— are masses of rags, and it would be hard to say which of the two was the most ragged.

His trowsers are better; but one leg reaches to the ground and the other has worn off nearly half way to the knee,— leaving the end rather uneven and uninviting in appearance. His boots are always good and well polished, and his hat is in the same good condition. He wears good gloves, which fit as if they were made to order by a Parisian glover. His beard is of the style which is cultivated by the upper classes, and, as well as his hair, is always in the best condition.

This queer person is said to be well connected, and well off in every way. Some of his high relatives have offended him, and he has taken this extraordinary course to shame and annoy them. Persons in carriages, on horseback and on foot, bow to him, and he returns the bow in a style which could not be excelled by a Duke. This extraordinary way he has been known to follow for nearly one-half of his life, and will probably continue in the same way during the remainder of it.

Sometimes he changes his clothes, but the new suit is a little more ragged than the old one, and it is a wonder to every one, where he obtains these clothes. He must have a process only known to himself of reducing ordinary clothes to rags, or else he has made a contract with a paper mill or an old clothes shop, to supply him with his wardrobe. If ever this gentleman should be in reduced circumstances, he might hire himself to a rag shop, for a sign or for a sort of figure-head to that institution.

There is a retired physician, who sometimes, but rarely, walks in Kensington Gardens,— adjoining Hyde Park, who is rather in an advanced age, but in good health, walking easily and firmly.

He wears black tight-fitting trowsers, and high top boots, and he invariably wears a fox-skin cap with the tail of the fox hanging down behind. He is a very modest man, of quiet appearance, who, when he sees people who are looking at him, blushes,— hurries forward, and is very much embarrassed.

He clings to his fox-skin cap with the tail, and to his top boots. Once he was compelled to appear as a witness, in some law Court in the City, and when he entered the Court room there was a considerable laughter at his appearance; and he was more embarrassed than ever. He wore his cap until he was desired to remove it, which he did with some reluctance. A few years ago he had a good practice, but something went wrong with him, and he has avoided society since he gave up his profession.

Another person is drawn, on a Bath chair, over the walks in the Park, by a servant in livery. This person is a young man, thirty years old, unable to walk from paralysis, or from some complaint depriving him of the use of his limbs.

His face is painted as white as the face of a clown in a circus, or a pantomime, and his eyebrows and eyelashes, are daubed with some black material, which, contrasting with the white on his face,— gives him a very strange and rather a hideous look. Every policeman he sees he insists on shaking by the hand, and telling them that they must be sure to call at his residence.

He thinks that the policemen are great men and have entire control of the Government, and as he is somewhat ambitious, hopes by their means to obtain a high position for himself. This person, in passing over the walks near Rotten Row, frequently raises his hat, when ladies are near, and bows and smiles, as if the ladies were his most intimate friends.

He, with his chair and servant in livery, travels over the entire part of England, — visiting all of the best watering-places in the summer, and Bath and Cheltenham in the winter. His face is always painted white, and his eyebrows and lashes are covered with black material; nothing can induce him to arrange his appearance in a more rational manner.

VI.

THEATRICALS EXTRAORDINARY.

MADAME BERNHARDT has finished her season in London — having been well patronized. Few English people who saw her, understand French, for, as a class — they have no inclination for that language. An old English gentleman in a restaurant in Paris — asked a waiter for an English newspaper — speaking in Anglo-French, and the waiter replied, "yes, sur; what paper, sur?" When the English tourists go to the Continent with their bundles of canes and umbrellas, thick boots, field glasses, and long veils, they should take their language also with them, excepting — the letter A, which might be safely stowed away at home, until they return to the land of Southdowns.

If Madame Bernhardt goes to America, she will be well received, and well patronized, and her visit will be pleasant and remunerative.

In a town in the north of England, a few years ago, a shoemaker forsook the last of the temple of St. Crispin, for his first and last appearance at the temple of St. Thespis. He was a small, miserable, half-starved looking person, with a falsetto voice, beginning with a bass and ending with a soprano. The play was "The Lady of the Lake," and he was James Fitz James. In the first scene was the hero near the bold cliffs of the Trosachs with Loch Katrine near by, and his horse dead: —

> "Woe worth the chase, woe worth the day,
> That cost thy life, my gallant gray."

Then he attempted to blow his horn, but the instrument would not toot; and he was relieved by the orchestra. Pretty soon the Lady of the Lake made her appearance, and he

> "Stood concealed amid the brake, to view this Lady of the Lake."

As the boat came near it suddenly stopped, and Ellen came very near being upset. She was undoubtedly very angry, and looked as if she could have smashed the little skiff, and everything connected with it. She was a firm, healthy-looking damsel: —

> "What though the sun, with ardent frown,
> Had slightly tinged her cheek with brown," —

At any rate, Ellen looked as if the mountain air agreed with her.

> "What though upon her speech there hung
> The accents of the mountain tongue."

James Fitz James accompanies the fair Ellen to the rustic bower, where he remained sometime, but when he wanted to leave the bower he could not find the door, and hunted around for it. When he found it he could not open it, and finally gave a knock, and it was opened from the other side. Poor Blanche of Devon appeared shot by an arrow; and after Fitz James had "finished" Murdoch of Alpine, which he did after some sharp running, with considerable clattering and noise of broadswords, Red Murdoch was large enough to take up James and carry him off, but he kindly went down at the right time, and the hero returns to assist Blanche.

"She sate beneath the birchen tree,
Her elbow resting on her knee;"

She was a lady weighing apparently fifteen stone, and she and Fitz James had forgotten their parts, for she threw herself into his arms — and he, unable to support her weight and bulk, dropped her to the ground — when she gave the hero a look which made him tremble.

James Fitz James finally encounters the terrible Roderick Dhu, and when several heads appear at Roderick's whistling, he flourished his sword in a new way and said,

> "Come one, come hall; this rock shall fly
> From hits firm base has soon has hi,"

his voice underwent several changes during this warlike challenge. Roderick was a tremendous fellow, evidently well acquainted with Southdown mutton, Yorkshire hams, and Devonshire cream — if he did live in Scotland. After the combat with the swords, when Roderick caught James by the throat he choked him well, and James twisted and squirmed like a little serpent, until Roderick fainted, and when James Fitz James recovered his sword, it seemed at first as if he would have hit him on the head several times to pay him off for the choking. When James Fitz James attends fair Ellen in his place, the former shows considerable embarrassment, for a King in his own palace, when

> "To him each lady's look was lent.
> Midst furs, and silks, and jewels sheen,
> He stood in simple Lincoln green."

Malcolm was the best actor, and the best-looking person on the stage, and the King was evidently jealous of him, and drew the chain of gold rather tight.

> "Then gently drew the glittering band,
> And laid the clasp on Ellen's hand."

The curtain here descended.

VII.

A MUSEUM VISITOR.

THERE is a man in London who is more eccentric than any other person mentioned in these sketches. He is apparently fifty years old, under the medium height, and very slim.

I have seen him at various times for a number of years, and he always looks the same as he did when I first saw him.

Winter and summer he wears a very heavy, black overcoat, rather the worse for use, trowsers of the same color of the coat, more worn than the latter, and a hat in a worse state than either, which was drawn down to his neck behind, and brought his ears out beyond the narrow brim, giving him an appearance entirely different from any other human being.

His heavy boots are of the style known in England as that which never wear out, but are worn by one person during his life and then taken up by another, and so on until they are burned up or lost.

The first time that I saw this partially shabby-genteel man, was when I was in the British Museum, ten years ago. I was looking at the fine collection of stuffed birds — the best that I ever saw — when I heard a loud sound, as if some fair-sized cart horse was travelling over the floor, and, as the noise approached, I heard a voice saying, in rather a sharp tone: "Birds, parrots, ducks, eagles," etc. And this man appeared walking very fast—almost at a run—making a terrible noise with his boots, and every thing in the Museum that he saw and had time to name rapidly, he did. He walked rapidly through every room in the Museum, and never ceased his private conversation.*

When he had finished his tour of inspection, he rushed out of the building into the street, and went onward at a very fast walk for a man.

The next time that I saw him, was in Victoria Park, some months afterwards, with the same clothes, and walking at the same rate of speed. He was now accompanied by a dog of the cur order, which at one time might have been of the size of a good-sized fox hound, but care and want had apparently reduced his size.

* AUTHOR'S NOTE. — He came to some antiquities and said, "mummy, sarcophagus," etc.

This dog, like his master, had no feeling of friendship for any of his fellow beings. As he followed his master, he would first raise one hind leg, and then after resting the leg for a few moments, would drop it to the ground and raise the other, and so he continued to do, until he disappeared with his master.

As the dog's master passed the seat which I occupied, at his usual pace, he said, "Grass, trees, flowers, benches," etc., until I could no longer hear his voice. When he visits Parks and all out of door places, he is accompanied by his dog; but when he visits Museums, galleries, or the inside of any buildings, he leaves his dog at home. I once saw him in St. Paul's, when he was going at his usual pace; but suddenly he stopped and pulling a piece of paper from his pocket, he began to make figures with a pencil, and as he did so he muttered: "Nineteen from eleven leaves six; fifty goes into twenty-seven twice and one to carry; aught added to aught makes twenty five;" and then having finished his arithmetical calculations, he thrust the paper and pencil into his pocket and rushed for the street.

I had not seen this gentleman for a long time; had lost sight of him in fact. But one evening in the early autumn, as I was standing near the Serpentine, I heard a heavy, quick walk, followed by a sharp, quick voice, and immediately I knew what was coming. As the pedestrian pilgrim passed at his swiftest pace, he said, "Serpentine, swans, fish;" and on he went, almost leaping in his quick retreat from the Park. The dog was close to his heels, neither looking to the right nor to the left, but just raising one leg and then the other, with a little more rapidity of motion, and rather more often than he did when I last saw him, and with such a wretched, sad, downcast, starved look, that I always think of him whenever I see a dog of his size.

* * * * * *

There is a gentleman, apparently infirm in body, who, in the most pleasant part of the year, is drawn in a bath-chair, by a servant in livery, while another servant, also in livery, walks by his side. I should suppose the gentleman to be in age about sixty years. He is rather large, well dressed, and he would not attract any person or repel them, by his appearance. But he always has six dogs tied to his chair, with cords, each about six feet long. Each dog represents his tribe, with the exception of one, who is a cur.

One day, as this gentleman was taking his customary airing, those dogs, (severally of the grayhound, terrier, pug, King Charles, poodle and cur tribes,) got somewhat entangled in the cords by which they were led. Some of them wished to go forward, some backward, and some were determined to go crossways. They became rather confused, and the cur began to bark. As soon as he made this disagreeable noise, every dog in the pack followed his example, and very soon other dogs near, hearing the noise, also began to bark and to hurry to the scene of the uproar. As fresh dogs arrived, they naturally wished to know the cause of the commotion; but not being properly informed, became angry, and thought they would annihilate the entire lot. Then began a series of barkings, growlings, howlings and yelpings, as were not often heard there or in any other place. Most of the dogs became entangled in the leading strings which were fastened to the vehicle, and it required several policeman and laborers to separate the animals, and to place the pets in their customary positions.

* * * * * *

Five or six years ago, two poor Frenchmen had a dancing bear which they were leading around London.

They would stop in a street near the corner of a great thoroughfare, and one of the Frenchmen would play a violin and the bear would dance — going through extraordinary movements — sometimes jumping nearly fifteen feet, jingling the bells around his neck, and growling in a very disagreeable way at the same time. When I saw him, it was nearly night, and he had climbed to the top of a lamp-post, and had opened the door to the light, or broken the glass. He put his nose to the light, which burnt him in a miserable manner, for he bellowed in a terrific voice, dropping to the ground, first standing on his head, and then upon his hind legs, and rubbing his nose with his fore paw. Several women and children were badly frightened, and horses would not come any where near the animal. Policemen tried to arrest the owners of the bear; but he turned on them, and they ran for dear life, the bear taking their clubs in many instances, and giving them to his masters. It seemed at one time, that it would require an entire police force to arrest the bear and his masters; but finally a rope with a noose was thrown over the animal and he was secured, and his masters were arrested.

VIII.

THE DESERTED ROOM.

TEN years ago an old gentleman often visited Rotten Row, in a carriage drawn by a single horse, which was driven by a middle-aged man, dressed in a plain way, and entirely without the distinctive marks which usually accompany persons in his position. The proprietor of the carriage was a fine-looking man, and would, by any one, be classed as a person belonging to the extreme upper classes.

This gentleman would be driven into the main road for carriages, where the coachman would stop. The master would then leave the carriage, and, after walking and sitting for an hour or more, would enter his carriage and leave the Park.

He was seen to converse with persons of nearly his age and apparent position, who were conversant with his history.

A tale told by a number of persons may, like the scene of a drama, become impaired by time; but, by being repainted by new artists, the old scenery looks as well as it did when it was new. Some people are particular in describing the localities when any event of importance occurs, and the house and room were well known for a long time where an interesting event occurred.

For about fifty years there was a house in the olden part of London, which (with the exception of one room in the front second story), was always occupied; but that room, by the order of the owner of the house, was to be kept closed, and no one to enter it, or attempt to do so, either from the inside or from the outside of the dwelling. These commands were obeyed, and he who gave them was the old gentleman with the one-horse carriage and driver, who sometimes visited Hyde Park.

This gentleman had been left, at an early age, without parents or relations, but with a number of warehouses and dwelling-houses, and a good supply of ready money. He was good-looking, sensible and well-educated; and was of good birth, wealthy, of good abilities and popular. Combining all of these advantages, it would appear to persons of the past and of the present time that he could have been surpassed by very few young men in London, or in England.

When he came into the possession of his property, he employed a respectable old lady for a housekeeper. She was occasionally visited by a young and a very beautiful lady, who had lived in a family where the old lady had been an upper servant or housekeeper; and the younger person, as was perfectly natural, when she was on good terms with the older one, would sometimes come and have a nice, quiet chat with her old friend.

This young lady was entirely without relations or fortune, and with very few acquaintances among those of her own sex. She was well-educated and accomplished, and possessed a large amount of firmness, self-esteem and self-reliance. Her guardian or instructor must have trained her well, for she always managed to be ahead of every one of her own sex that she came in contact with.

She taught French, Italian and music, which gave her a good income, and enabled her to gratify her tastes for dress, and occasionally take short tours on the Continent, and to the favorite places of resort in England.

Whenever she came into a drawing-room, or in any place where ladies and gentlemen were assembled, the ladies (irrespective of position) had to stand aside and take a back seat, while the better part of the male portion would hover around, and the smaller portion would only look at her with admiration. In regard to the female part of the company, she cared no more for them than she did for her pupils, and not, in reality, so much; for she lived out of her pupils, and knew that she must praise and conciliate them, whether they were stupid or not.

Can any one blame this person for her independent ways, when she knew that there was not a single lady in England or on the Continent, that she had met, who would not hesitate for a moment to crush her, as they would a venomous insect, under their feet? It was not her fault if men left their elder lady acquaintances and came to her; for she might wear a dress entirely out of fashion, and it would be the same with the men who would follow her; and it was not to be wondered at that they did so, for she was evidently above any young lady whom they met.

The owner of the house, when this young lady came to see his housekeeper, gave the old lady permission to receive her visitors in the drawing-room of the second floor front; and even insisted that she should do so, as she was a gentlewoman, if she was a housekeeper, and those who called to visit her were people who were worthy of being received in the drawing-room.

One day this gentleman entered the drawing-room when the young lady was there, and, of course, was introduced to her, and in a few days was engaged to be married to her; the proposal being made and accepted in that drawing-room.

The gentleman was undoubtedly very much attached to the young lady, but it always appeared to him that she was not entirely satisfied with the contract, and when the day was to be named for the marriage ceremony, that she hesitated, and finally named the day in an indifferent manner.

The appointed day having arrived, and the ceremony having been completed, the bride and her husband, with the invited guests, assembled in the drawing-room, in which the breakfast had been laid out. The bride afterwards appeared in her traveling dress, ready for the usual tour on the Continent.

About this time a young man of a foreign appearance was looking in the direction of the room in the second story. He was looking intently, with a sad but sometimes savage expression of countenance. His dress was of good materials, but was certainly not in a good condition, as it was from head to foot spotted with mud. He wore top boots and spurs, as if he had recently dismounted from a horse — which he had probably done, as railways were not then known. He looked like one who had ridden for a long distance without rest, and for some great purpose, arriving too late, and being weary, sad, ill and disappointed, he may have felt and looked a little savage.

Probably at that time he was disgusted with life, and, although he has been described as rather tall and very handsome, he could not at that time have been very attractive in appearance.

The bride, as she was drawing on her gloves, looked into the street and started back with a slight scream, but in almost a moment turned to the guests, and said, "Look there, do you see that man? he is the only one that I love, or have loved, or ever can love;" and then she almost tore the chain from her neck, the bracelets from her arms, and the rings from her fingers, and taking some keys from her pocket, dashed them with the jewelry on the table, and turning to her husband said, "In my boxes you will find everything you have given me." Without waiting for a reply, she rushed from the room, down the stairs, and into the street. When she ran to the young man, he started back with a look first of surprise, and soon of pleasure. She caught him by the hand, and it seemed as if she would have thrown her arms around his neck, but she was too discreet to make too great a scene at that time and place.

A cab was near at the right time, when she called to the driver, and opening the door, partly pushed the young man into it, and then, with a few hurried words to the driver, entered the vehicle, which was driven rapidly away. Since that time it has never been known where this determined lady and her companion went, where they lived, or whether they may now be living.

The forsaken husband turned to his guests, (who were stupefied with wonder,) saying, "My friends — if I may call all of you so, (and he looked at his housekeeper, who turned pale, trembled and looked downwards,) in this room I have been the most happy and wretched person who has ever entered it, and from this day no human being shall enter it during my life."

The guests soon departed, and the door leading to the room was securely fastened. Everything, including the table with its contents, was left in the room, and the blinds were left as they were when they were partially drawn by the young bride when she saw her adored standing on the pavement in the street, and with that look which can only be possessed by a disappointed man.

The house was always occupied with the exception of that one room, but the owner lived there no more, and rarely saw the house, or even went into the street where it was situated.

As may be supposed, the house with the deserted room was a curiosity for several years, but in fifty years great changes take place. About nine years ago a fire consumed three houses, including the house with the deserted room, in the old part of London.

IX.

SWELLS AND CANINES.

THERE are two young gentlemen who are inseparable companions. One may be alone for a short time, but the other is sure to find him, to the mutual satisfaction of both.

They are considerably under the medium size, and dress enough alike to be taken for twins, if their features were not entirely opposed to each other. The mouth of one is nearly on one side of his face, as if it was trying to reach his ear, while the mouth of the other is in front, but it takes a diagonal direction, as if it was dissatisfied with the line across, and was endeavoring to reach the perpendicular. These young gentlemen walk, drive and ride; in either amusement always wearing lemon colored gloves, and flowers fastened to their coats. They are seen at the opera, theatres, and every other place of amusement. I once saw them in Switzerland.

They do not appear to have any lady acquaintances; but at the Opera make frequent use of their glasses;

and very rarely fail to applaud at the right time, but, if they should make such a mistake, the speed with which the opera glasses are passed to their eyes, removes the greater part of their embarrassment.

Both of these young persons sometimes adopt the style of languid swells, and their manners and way of speaking are very entertaining.

One fine morning one of them was on horseback in Rotten Row, where he was soon joined by the other, who said, "Wery good morning Hawvy. I did not see you at the opawa last night."

The other replied, "Well no, you see, I wasn't there, you know, because I dined at seven, you know; and I couldn't go, you see." Then these two leaders of society rode on.

It is hardly rational to think that these two friends can always be friendly and loving to each other; like birds in their little nests agreeing, including the doves.

All of these birds do not always agree, for I have seen some wretched fights among them. A very few creatures in the world always agree, for such has never been the state of affairs, and it is rather late in the day for a change.

Sometime ago, these loving young persons procured

a couple of dogs, one of them a greyhound, the other a large animal of no particular race. One day in the autumn, when the visitors to the Park were few, these gentlemen, with their dogs, were walking in one of the paths, when a misunderstanding occurred with the dogs, which ended by the larger one making an attempt as if to devour the other! The two friends interfering, for a short time, were not friends, but their dogs were separated, and they all were reconciled.

X.

FRENCH PEOPLE.

THE people in England are grieved by the untimely death of the Prince Imperial, and by the inglorious manner in which his life was sacrificed. A large number of all classes, blame the officer, who, as it is reported, had charge of the party and the Prince, at the time of the sad occurrence.

Others think that the Prince himself was to blame for exposing himself in such a useless way; some think that he should not have been allowed to go on such an irregular expedition, and others say he ought not to have gone to South Africa, at all.

The last opinion is probably the most rational one, and will in course of time, be the opinion of every one, who has an opinion of his own, and is not afraid to express it.

The ex-Empress is receiving general sympathy, and the memory of the ill-fated young man will be respected for her sake; for the respect that the people of England had for his father; and, it may be, for the admiration they have for the talents that his great uncle possessed; who was once feared, rather more than admired.

Whatever may have been the defects of the first Napoleon in a moral point of view, all must admit that uniting in one man the qualities of a general, a man of business, and a ruler, he was the greatest that the world ever saw, and it will not be very rash to say that no Bonaparte will ever attempt to even emulate the first Napoleon.

There was some controversy a few years ago, about the manner of Napoleon's treatment at St. Helena. Opinion was, of course, divided, but many thought he had been treated well; some thought he had been treated as well as he deserved; some said a good deal better, while a few quietly said that he did not receive the treatment that a great, but unfortunate man should have received in a similar situation.

Undoubtedly a large number of people in England regret that the Government of sixty-four years ago, did not allow the wife, or any of Napoleon's relations or friends to accompany him in his exile, some of them to remain with him for a short time, for he was almost alone, and the contemplation of his situation preyed on his mind, while a painful disease, created by months of inactivity, preyed upon his body. He was almost chained to a rock, the world above gave him no ray of hope, and the sea which surrounded him, brought him no tidings of comfort; while his life was ebbing away.

There is a portion of history of the heathen mythology, which seems applicable to Napoleon's situation at St. Helena.

Jupiter was the supreme god of the Roman Pagan world, and all things, animate and inanimate, were supposed to exist by his will. Mercury was the deity who was delegated by Jupiter to convey those who were condemned to the Infernal regions. Prometheus excelled all of the others in knowledge, and was the one who made images of clay, formed like men, and to animate them into things of life, procured celestial fire, which was applied to the images, and they became living souls.

Jupiter was informed of the act of Prometheus, and sent Mercury to hurl him from Heaven. Mercury obeyed the order of his superior, and Prometheus, by the commands of Jupiter, was chained to a rock on the sea shore, and there was left to be devoured by vultures.

Jupiter saw with pleasure the blood-stained body and bloody sweat of his rival, and heard with delight his death cries of agony.

Prometheus had been insulted, tortured and murdered, and his name was forever erased from the books of the Pagan Heaven.

The screaming of the ravenous birds, in their horrible banquet, and the moaning of the sad sea waves, were his only requiem.

Justice, according to the laws of the gods, was satisfied; revenge was satiated, and Jupiter reigned without a rival.

If the people of France wish to maintain their republic, they should abolish titles, for a monarchical republic, and a republican monarchy, cannot permanently exist.

France claims to be a first-class republic, and at the same time there are persons in that republic who call themselves Dukes, Counts, Princes, etc., and their titles are recognized by nearly all of the Republicans!

XI.

THE ENGLISH.

SOME of the people here say that England is a republican monarchy. England is no such thing, for the Queen is an hereditary sovereign, and the members of the House of Lords are hereditary legislators, and also are possessed of considerable power, which they can use, when they think proper to do so.

The Princess of Wales drives in the Park, (during the greater part of the parlimentary season,) every day. In the morning from twelve to two she drives a beautiful pair of iron gray horses, harnessed to a phaeton, is accompanied by a lady-friend, and very often she rides in the afternoon. She also rides on horseback, sometimes in the morning. The Prince of Wales is often seen riding in the Park, or in Rotten Row; which is all the same, and all members of the Royal family ride and drive in the Park, as much, or probably more, than those who are not royal.

The family carriages of the members of the Royal family, are like those used in New York, and other

American cities, but the coachmen and footmen wear liveries far more showy than are seen in the American cities, with the addition of powdered hair, sometimes white wigs curled like those of the judges, and of lawyers who are Queen's counsel. Sometimes when the Queen arrives or departs from Buckingham Palace, generally accompanied by the Princess Beatrice — her carriage is drawn by four horses with outriders, and escorted by a portion of the guards on horseback. But her Majesty does not reside in London, for three weeks, during the entire year.

The old palace of Hampton Court, which was built by Cardinal Woolsey during the reign of Henry the Eighth, is occupied by titled families, who have been unfortunate in a monetary point of view, and are allowed to occupy the Palace free of rent. They endeavor to make the same show as others who have the necessary amount of money to procure the luxuries of life, but the attempt is evidently a failure.

A short time ago, a lady with the title of Viscountess, who was very poor, and supported herself by making clothes for a tailor, was by her friends placed in a comfortable condition. She had supported herself in this way for a number of years, until she was taken ill, and being over seventy years of age; was found in a starving condition.

It is true that people who are in distress, can always be relieved at the work-houses, but there are people who will starve, rather than to so humiliate themselves.

Three years ago in London, or three years from last winter, two sisters were found in a miserable room, dead — with no fire, food or bed in the room. They were known to be entirely destitute, and were urged to go to a work-house, but refused, and being unable to obtain work as needle-women, preferred to starve, rather than in any way to beg.

The asylums for the poor or for those who cannot procure work, and for those who are unable to work, do a great deal of good, and some harm, as there are persons who will not work, as long as they can live without the same, and be supported by the Government. It is true that most of the asylums for the poor, compel the inmates to do some kind of work, but the products of their labors are not of much use to any one.

An old man was found in a work-house last winter, who was born there, married there, and had several of his children born there.

It is very evident that if there were not so many of

these institutions, the poor would emigrate and support themselves in some other countries, and become independent.

A large number of persons in England are brought very low by the whiskey and gin which they drink; and a great many spend more for drink than they do for bread, meat and other necessaries; and by following this habit for a few years, become unfit for every kind of work, and end their lives in the poor-houses.

The drinking establishments are in every part of London, by thousands, and women drink as well as men, and sometimes the children do the same. The beer and stout that they drink may not do them much harm, but some of the whiskey and gin is the vilest stuff that has ever been made in any country, since they were first made.

Brewers and distillers make large fortunes, and sometimes make good use of their money. Sometimes, undoubtedly, the distillers make good spirits; but if the reports are true, the greater part of what is sold in the ordinary drinking shops in London, is unfit for use, and those who use it, show by their looks that it is killing them. The same, but not to the same extent, can be said of those who use to excess a better quality of the same.

The people here say that the weather is so cold, rainy and uncertain, that they require stimulants, and must have them. It may be that beer and porter are beneficial to them, for both are said to be generally unadulterated, and the brewers are well-known and popular men.

* * * * * *

Since the Americans have sent fresh beef to this country, there is great complaint that the butchers charge the same for it that they do for the best English and Scotch beef, and thus wrong the people by this unfair course.

The people have been informed by the dealers in meat, that beef is sold at prices which vary according to the quality, and according to the law of supply and demand. If American beef is as good or better than other beef, it will be sold at the same, or better prices, than other beef sells for.

American cotton brings a better price than the cotton of other countries, because it is better, and the same rule will apply to beef and all other necessaries of life.

* * * * * *

The farmers in England are having the most severe

trials they ever had. The wheat and hay crops are entire failures, owing to months of wet weather. They cannot raise oxen, sheep and pigs at remunerative prices, are behind in paying their rents, and do not know what to do, for the future appears to them as discouraging as the present. No one, not living here, can have the most remote idea of the farmers' troubles.

I saw a letter from a farmer who lives in the west of England, and after speaking of his great troubles, ends his letter by hoping that the powers above would help the English farmers, for they can not help themselves.

* * * * * *

It is quite probable that the emigration to the Colonies, and to the United States, from England, will be very large for several years; and it would be much larger, if the poorer classes could raise enough money to pay for their passages to any country beyond the seas.

XII.

A BATCH OF ARTISANS.

NEAR the roads for the carriages and equestrians, and by the walks in Hyde Park, is a large number of benches, which may be occupied free, and are generally filled when the visitors to the Park are in great numbers.

Seated on one of these benches were five men, who, by their dress and conversation, would be classed as belonging to the order known in America as mechanics, but here are sometimes called artisans. If a man here is a blacksmith, carpenter, or a bricklayer, he is a *mechanic;* but if he is engaged in finer work, he is an *artisan.* I confess that it is rather difficult for me (to use a familiar expression) to draw the line — about as difficult as to explain why a servant who drives horses should be called *a driver*, and when his master takes the reins, that the latter should become *a whip.* The latter is a mystery to all people—who are not English.

The five persons on the bench may have belonged to the artisan class, but it is my opinion that they belonged to the order of mechanics. One of them, who was called Jones, was explaining to the others the principles of a very remarkable contrivance, where a man, by placing one of his fingers on a lever, could raise a body weighing one hundred tons or more, as easily as a man could raise a pewter pint pot of porter to his lips, and said that this great machine was the invention of himself, and of no one else.

Three of the party seemed to be very much interested about the elevator, when the pint of porter was mentioned, and looked, and probably thought, that they would have no objection to make a trial, at that time, of the elevator and the porter — provided that each one of them could have before him a pint pot of porter, and to be allowed to elevate the porter before testing the wonderful powers of the great labor-saving machine.

One of them remarked that if Mr. Jones could perfect his invention, and secure himself by the necessary patent, his fortune would be made in a very short time.

One of the party, whose name was Sanders, was a little skeptical in regard to the invention, and said in plain words that he did not believe in Jones or his invention, and that Jones was a humbug.

On hearing this view of himself and his wonder of the world, Jones immediately rose from the bench, and, inserting the nose of Sanders between his thumb and first finger, proceeded to pinch that useful organ very energetically; then, giving it a sudden twist, the scrutinizer of odors was nearly turned upside down, or downside up; and next, with the rapidity of thought, Jones raised the pedestal of his right limb in such a manner, that Sanders was nearly raised from the ground, and propelled forward several feet with considerable velocity, while Mr. Jones stopped to recover his breath.

In this way Jones was enabled to explain and illustrate to Sanders the main workings of his invention, which was nothing more nor less than a combination of the vice, screw and lever, and in reality very simple.

Sanders appeared to object to the manner of Jones' explanation; and when he had recovered from the surprise and mortification that he was placed in by the superior argumentative powers of Jones, proceeded to put a plan which he had hastily formed into immediate execution.

Sanders belonged to the old school, and believed that bodies, either heavy or light, could be lowered much easier than they could be raised; so, to prove and support this theory, he brought his right hand to bear to the centre of Jones' face.

A principle has been promulgated by scientific men that when an animate body comes into collision with an inanimate one, and both are of equal size, the inanimate body must go down, and is injured more or less, according to the velocity of the movable object.

This theory was then shown to be a correct one in the case of Sanders *vs.* Jones, and Jones went down.

About this time several policemen made their appearance on the scene. Messrs. Jones and Sanders left the Park in their company, followed by their three friends and some others.

XIII.

BENHAFIT AND A BEAR STORY.

THERE is a famous individual in England who calls himself Benhafit the Prophet, who has not made his appearance in the Park, but his advent is daily expected. He is small in size, dresses entirely in sheepskins, and at a distance of six hundred yards somewhat resembles a gigantic southdown on his hind legs.

Some time ago he was in a town in the south of England, and gave notice that he would preach on a certain day, in a vacant place near the town. When the time came for Benhafit to appear, a large number of people had assembled, composed of men, women and children of all ranks and professions. Some came to see and hear the preacher, and some came to annoy him.

After Benhafit had spoken for a short time, and had spoken well, the pickpockets, (like some other professional persons in an Arcadian country) became eager for clients, and the crowd were getting noisy, a policeman made his appearance, who desired the preacher to "move hon," and I regret to record the fact that Benhafit so far forgot himself and calling and pretensions as to make use of language which was not becoming for a man in his profession to use. He turned to the policeman and said: "What do you mean, you poorly-paid, half-starved plebeian hireling, to speak to a gentleman, telling him to move on? Do you know who I am, and what my pretensions are?" Then he gave the policeman a look which ought to have terrified him, but it did not seem to have much effect upon the guardian of the peace. As Benhafit would not "move *hon*," he was moved *hoff*, and locked up for a night for disturbing the peace, and brought before a justice in the morning, lectured, admonished, and dismissed with the usual caution. He then went to his hotel, and asked permission from the landlord to make an address to the people who were present, the main room of the building being well filled with people who came to see and hear this remarkable man.

Benhafit then said that he did not care for judges, justices, lawyers, policemen, or any other biped or quadruped, or for anything animate or inanimate in this detestable, deceitful world. He said he was traveling through the country, endeavoring to do some good by his preaching, good example, and strictly temperate habits. The more and better he preached, the worse the people acted, and treated him badly, almost without exception. He said, sometimes when he was in the middle of his oration, and he thought he had made a good and lasting impression, some imp would imitate the squealing of a pig, the quacking of a duck, the barking of a dog, the crowing of a cock, or some other wretched, clownish noise, and he had hoped that when these manifestations of dissent were made by a lot of clowns, the better part of his audience would eject these wretches; but, instead of doing so, they encouraged them by their laughter to continue their vulgar noises, and he was very often compelled to desist from continuing his discourse, because his audience could not hear him; and then his discourse, which he had prepared by great mental labor and research, was almost useless, and he had concluded at one time to leave this country, and not to return; but all countries were bad, and it always seemed to him that every new place that he visited, was much worse than the last one, and he wished a good-sized earthquake would swallow up everything, world and all.

Benhafit, in continuing to mention his grievances,

said that, if he was not following his profession, he would wish to be a judge, for he would hang every criminal he could lay his hands on; for, if they went into prison for a few years, they were ten times worse when their term of imprisonment expired than they were before they were convicted.

He was disgusted, he declared, with everything in general, and with the world in particular. For a number of years he had lived alone in a hut in the woods, and in a distant country, and the only friend and companion he had during his retirement was a fine dog, who was killed by a large black bear. The dog attacked the bear, who raised himself on his hind legs and gave his dog a cuff on the side of his head, and that faithful follower and friend was instantly placed *hors de combat*. He fired the contents of his rifle at the abominable beast, but, having missed him, was compelled to run to escape the embrace of the savage animal; and, having reached his house and closed and fastened the door, soon saw the head of the animal at the window, which he appeared to be entering, and he caught up a kettle of boiling water which he had intended for culinary purposes, and threw the same into the face of the savage beast, who instantly dropped from the window and ran away, making horrible bellowings, and rubbing his nose and head on the ground, to alleviate the pain, and he turned several complete summersaults, and continued howling, roaring and bellowing until he was out of sight.

He thought that he had seen the last of the bear, but early on the following day he heard a scratching on the side of his house, and then on the roof, and knew that the animal intended to reach him by descending the chimney. So he seized his double-barrelled shot-gun, which was always ready for use, and fired the contents at the bear's head, after the beast had entered the chimney, which nearly blew the animal's head into pieces, and caused him to descend, bringing with him a large amount of soot, which greatly injured some bread, meat and potatoes which he had intended to use for his day's repast.

The bear's skin was used for constructing a suit of clothes, which he wore during his remaining stay in the woods; but since he had lived among people who called themselves civilized he had dressed in sheep-skins, as he thought that such a dress was more appropriate than the bear-skin, as the former was emblematical of peace; but, from his experience in this country, he feared that he should have to again enter his bear-skin suit.

Benhafit then made a bow worthy of a duke, and left the room, and, shortly after, the town.

XIV.

ENGLAND AND AMERICA.

I SHALL now endeavor to give an idea of the opinions of the people in England, in regard to the tariff and the destiny of America.

All admit that America is a powerful, wealthy and prosperous country, with a large and increasing population, but they say "how long she will retain these advantages, remains to be seen."

A medical man remarked to me, when we were speaking of America, that it was true that she had a large and increasing population, but at some time the immigration would nearly cease, and then the population, instead of increasing, would retrograde.

This gentleman was then informed of the number of people in the States one hundred years ago, and the number now, deducting the immigrants who had arrived in that time, and the population acquired by the purchase of Florida, Louisiana, Texas, New Mexico and California. He said he had always been informed that the descendants of the older population were decreasing in numbers, and he was now informed that every town of any importance, and nearly every county in the United States, had more or less persons, living in those parts, who were born in the New England or Middle States.

* * * * * *

The people in England have, as may be supposed, but one idea in regard to the American tariff, and are mostly in favor of Free Trade at home.

All say that it is not right for a man or woman in the States, to be compelled to pay more for a poorer article than can be furnished them from England, at a lower price.

The reply is that they must be in error, as America is selling goods to this country, to her colonies, and to other countries.

One remark they always make when they say that the high tariff has made America the dearest country in the world to live in, and it is intimated to them that they are rather short-sighted, as the United States have furnished the necessaries of life to a large part of the population of England, for a number of years, and have largely supplied them to a part of the population in every country, for a great many years, and considering the good quality and low prices of men's and women's wear, persons can live and dress cheaper in the United States, than they can in England, if they are so disposed.

Then they answer that, as they buy the products of the American soil, America ought to buy the English manufactures, meaning that the States should make no goods, but purchase of England, and the reply is that England would certainly buy nothing of America, if she could buy of other countries lower.

Then they repeat the old saying that Englishmen hold a large amount of American securities, as if they had purchased these securities to assist their dear friends, the Americans, and the answer is always the same, that they would not have bought these securities if they had not been good.

Then comes the last remark, when they say that England and America should be the best of friends, as they are in reality one people, speaking one language, and the two countries should go together, and help each other, as England is the mother of America.

At this last often repeated remark it is suggested to them that they are rather forgetful, for during our greatest trial, they allowed ships to leave England, armed and equipped, which, navigated by pirates, had nearly destroyed the American mercantile marine, which would have been the first in the world at the present time, but for those ships.

At that time the leading newspapers, even journals of the British government, advised the English people to have nothing to do with American bonds, and it was well known in America, that most of the manufacturers and merchants, as well as the wealthy and influential people in England, were almost universally in favor of the Union being broken. Of course they always say that the Union is too large, and that there must be at some time several governments, for the people, in various parts of the country, have various interests, and if the general Government will not gratify their wishes, then they will secede, and they point to the Governments of Europe, as an example. Their knowledge of the extent of some countries, must be limited, for Russia is twice as large as the United States,* (I mean the Russian empire,) and Brazil is nearly of the size of our country, while the

* The United States territory is not so large as many suppose, but large enough to entertain all the inhabitants in the above named countries.—*Author.*

British empire is more than three times the size of our country. The English people will be told by every intelligent and patriotic American, that the government of the United States is stronger than it has ever been; that if two, three or more States should endeavor to form a separate government, they could not succeed, for there is a power in America which is always strong enough to support the government, and to maintain the Union.

The form of the government might be changed several times, and the Union be maintained, and every mile of railway built in the States, makes the Union stronger than ever.

I will give my opinion about the tariff in America.

For the last thirty years the United States and her territories have produced a large part of the gold and silver which has been used by the civilized world, a large part of the cotton and tobacco, and, for several years, the United States have not had a strong competitor in furnishing any of the necessaries of life.

The United States can be entirely self-sustaining, and if the tariff twenty-five years ago had been one half of the rate of percentage of the tariff of the present time, a good part of the securities of the

United States, which are now held in Europe, would be held at home, and some of the gold in Europe, would be now in America, if she had properly protected herself, and the United States would by this time have been the money centre of the world.*

France understands the advantage of Protection, and does not allow many goods to enter the country, that they can make, for they believe in retaining their money, and other countries are following their example.

The old democratic free traders in America, never seemed to realize that other countries were getting rich at their expense. It seems a pity that the United States, with their splendid iron and coal deposits, should let them remain, until a short time ago, comparatively undeveloped, while they were paying scores of millions of dollars to England, for the most wretched railway iron that was ever made in any country.

The same, but not to the same extent, can be said about cotton and woollen goods, and other manufactured goods.

A country, to be permanently successful, must be permanently self-sustaining.

* There may be an inflation of gold in America in two years, which will be of more benefit to the country than an inflation of paper money.—*Author.*

XV.

CO-OPERATIVE STORES.

THERE are several co-operative stores in London, and the tradesmen of all denominations are making a great outcry against them, saying that these organizations are ruining their business, by selling articles of all kinds at wholesale prices, and sometimes at lower prices than tradesmen can purchase the same for; at least, some people say that such is the case.

The London tradesmen also say that large numbers of clerks are thrown out of employment, by establishing these new organizations, for the tradesmen are compelled to reduce their number of employés, as their business has fallen off, and they cannot afford to keep them.

All of this is doubtless true, but the general public is in favor of these new concerns, and think them a benefit to all who own shares in them.

They are joint-stock concerns, and none but shareholders can buy goods in them. Some of these stores do a large business, selling one million sterling, or more, per annum, and declaring good dividends to the share-holders, who are very well pleased with their investments, as they buy all of the goods they require at the stores, at very low rates, and receive a good interest on their money invested in shares.

These stores are now selling everything, including all kinds of provisions, and if they extend for the future, as they have extended in the past, the days of the high-price tradesmen are numbered, and they will be like the old stage coaches — things of the past.

The tradesmen ask the public, in a plaintive way, what they are to do, are advised to follow the examples of their former clerks, and obtain situations in the co-operative stores, and say that they would be unable to live on such small salaries; but they should be informed that their former clerks live on these small salaries, and some of them have splendid appetites.

The shopmen say that they have not been accustomed to live cheaply, and what they say may be true. Neither was one of their former clerks accustomed to live in splendor, when he had a large fortune left him, but he managed to exist.

The co-operative stores deliver no goods without

receiving cash for them, — they sell the best of everything and give employment to a large number of men.

As every customer is a share-holder, and is interested in the prosperity of these institutions, it would appear to all impartial persons,— that the success of these co-operative stores is, and must continue to be undoubted.

XVI.

BENHAFIT IN THE PARK.

BENHAFIT has at last made his long looked for, and much desired appearance in the Park, wearing his sheepskin dress, and followed and surrounded by a large and motley crowd of men, women and children. He paid little attention to them, and seemed to be in deep contemplation, as he walked slowly in the most unfrequented paths of the Park.

Now it appeared that nine or ten dogs, of all breeds, colors, dispositions, qualifications, and voices, who probably belonged to some of the people who were present, were following their owners about, and running and rolling on the grass, and enjoying themselves in their own way.

As these dogs came near Benhafit, and caught sight of his strange looks and dress, which would appear at the first sight to be a combination of the biped and quadruped, and looked like one of those strange mythological creatures, called Satyrs by the ancient pagans — two or three of the large dogs showed some signs of displeasure, by snarling, showing their teeth, and raising their hair on their backs, and one of the smaller dogs began to bark.

Now I have always observed, although it may have escaped the observation of persons who are more observant than myself, that when a dog, however insignificant, begins to bark, other dogs immediately follow his example, including those who compose one company, and all others who are within hearing, and I was not disappointed in this instance, for all of the others began to bark, making a complete chorus of music with the following voices, viz: Bass, baritone, tenor, alto, contralto, soprano, and falsetto,— the falsetto predominating.

The man of the sheepskin garment having awoke from his reverie, began to show some signs of fear, but the canine members of the extempore opera,— having yet committed no overt act,— he continued his walk, which appeared to be slightly faster, but the worst had yet to come.

In speaking of dogs, I omitted to mention another remarkable trait of that sagacious animal.

When a dog or any number of the same are in sight of any unusual commotion, they seem to have an irresistible desire to investigate the cause of the noise and uproar. The same may be said of individuals of a higher type of understanding.

The members of Benhafit's company of artists were joined by eight or ten more, of the same styles as the old company. On seeing this accession of strength, Benhafit was roused from his lethargy, and quickened his steps, and finally he began to run, and probably no man in a sheepskin dress, or a sheep itself,— ever ran faster than did Benhafit on this occasion.

The canine members of the opera now greatly increased in numbers and voices, were close to the preacher's heels, and kept up what may be called a running chorus, but I am happy to say that several policemen were near, and the poor bewildered man was rescued from his perilous position, and taken to an asylum, where he now rests; and it may be hoped that after his troublesome experience he may rest well.

Benhafit is not, as may be supposed, the name of this person, for he probably assumed the name when he was in Turkey or in some other part of the East. He is by birth an Englishman, and he was born near the Scottish border. His parents died when he had arrived at the age of manhood, and left him a small competence, which he has always managed to retain. He was a strange child from his birth, and when he began to learn to read, he was dull, and made but little advancement. But as he grew older he learned more readily and remembered everything that he had learned or read.

He rarely played with other boys, but when he did, excelled them in all kinds of pastime, as he excelled them in school.

He never was popular with any one, and the boys of his own age avoided him. When he was nearly a man in size and years, his parents endeavored to induce him to visit the people in the country near by them, for they did not live in a town, and he did so, but not willingly, and was finally induced to join a cricket club, and although there were few better players, he played but seldom, and finally quitted the club entirely.

He once attended a public meeting, and some of his acquaintances induced him to speak, and he did so, astonishing every one by his language and by his splendid delivery. All words seemed to be at his command, but when he had finished he never stayed to receive the congratulations of any one, but went directly home, and to his room, and remained there for several hours. He now became so silent, and at times so abstracted, that his parents feared that he would at the age of twenty be beyond their control, and entirely lost to them. He would take a book, and go into a field all by himself, and after reading for a short time, would drop the book, and gaze with an abstracted look upwards, as if he was trying to fathom the mysteries of space, and then he would suddenly look quickly and wildly about him, as if he was afraid of some one coming near him suddenly, and surprising him.

People now began to talk about him, and one day his parents were entertaining some friends in their humble way, and when their son came into the room, there was a look of surprise at his strange appearance.

Some few of the guests he had never met, and as he was introduced to them, they gave him one look of wonder, and then turned away. He was always a handsome person, but now although his face and features were good, insanity was lurking about him, and he knew of this, as soon, or sooner than any other person.

When the people looked at him and turned quickly away, he saw the look of surprise, and knew perfectly well, and he had probably known from his childhood that he was not like others, and when he became a youth, the dizziness, the aching of the head, and the confused ideas, told him that he was mad.

He was always kind. Children would stop in their play and come to him, while he had a kind word for all of them. Children in their mother's arms would throw up their hands with joy, and laugh and crow as he came near them. No dog would ever bite or even bark at him, until he wore his extraordinary dress, for he would speak to them and hold out his hand, when they would jump upon him, and lick his face and hands. When he went through the fields,—the cattle and sheep would come towards him. The birds would scarcely fly at his approach, and need not have done so, as he never killed any of them, but ofter threw them corn or crumbs of bread.

After his parents died, he went abroad for five years, traveling over the greater part of the Continent. He then returned to his old home, remaining there for only one year, and occupied his old room, where he stayed for the greater part of his visit.

He then went to Canada, where he lived all by himself in a forest, and where he had the adventure with the bear. In traveling in some parts of North America, he visited a camp-meeting, held by the Wesleyans, when he was induced to speak, and as he was admired by the persons present, he believed from that time that he was inspired.

Quos Deus vult perdere prius dementat.

XVII.

THE GENERAL'S FEATS.

THERE is no other part of the world, excepting Broadway, or the Bois de Boulogne, where such a variety of people are seen, as Hyde Park, near Rotten Row, in a pleasant day in May or June. The English place for recreation excels all others; and in fact, no other can be compared with it.

There is one little man who sometimes rides in Rotten Row, who by his appearance and the style of his horse, gets his share of attention. He is about five feet in height and weighs sixteen stone, and is said to be forty years of age, but might be one year younger or ten years older. He is a great hunter in the fox hunting season, and he goes from one meet to another, sometimes riding after the hounds three times in a single week, and the same horse is used in the majority of his hunting adventures, which enables him to be the first, or among the first, to be present at the death of the fox. He has been thrown from his horse a number of times, but has never been injured in the least.

His horse, who is called The General, is a queer looking animal — much taller than other horses — slim, with a neck like a dromedary's, and, when he is following the fox, or going at a fair rate of speed in Rotten Row, appears to be endeavoring to bring his nose on a line with the top of his neck.

He lost the greater part of one of his ears, by its having been bitten off by a bull-dog, as he had put his head into the dog's kennel to get a mouthful of straw which composed the ferocious animal's bed, and the other ear was cut off by his master to conform to the one already partially gone; but the good intentions on the part of his master were not realized — ending in a comparative failure.

The tail of this horse, either from age, accident or nature, has very little hair, and his mane is cut very close, and his back is rather low. He is a singular looking quadruped, and, when I first saw him, feeding in a pasture about ten miles from London, I could not determine what manner of beast he was. His color was different from any thing that I ever had seen — being a sort of reddish-black gray mixture, of no particular order, but a combination of several colors.

If any thing occurs during the pursuit of the fox,

when the rider of The General, intentionally or otherwise, (probably otherwise,) should be dismounted, the old horse goes straight forward, without paying the least attention to his master or rider, or to solicitations to halt, until the fox is caught, when he is perfectly quiet until his master appears on another horse, and either mounts The General or leads him home.

One day, in the late autumn, when the old horse and his rider were in a fair way to be the first to witness the termination of the day's sport, and the ending of the career of the animal who was said to be, at one time, rather fastidious as to the quality of grapes, they came to an elevated piece of ground and broad hedge, which caused the old hunter to stand almost upright on his hind legs, in order to gain the opposite side of the obstruction, and this movement caused his rider to go in a contrary direction from the course which both of them had been pursuing up to the time, successfully.

The General reached the other side of the hedge in safety, and not heeding the voice of his late rider, continued his course in the direction of the noise produced by the dogs, until he arrived at a river of about two hundred feet in width, with a rapid current; but he suddenly stopped for a moment, and then made a tremendous leap with the intention of reaching the opposite side of the river, but failed for once in his life, and fell into the river a few feet from the shore.

Having recovered from his surprise and immersion, he concluded to depart for the opposite bank; but the current was very swift and he was carried down the stream.

By this time a large part of the hunting party had arrived at the river, where they saw the veteran, or parts of him, descending the river, which was very rough and swift — almost a cataract. In a short distance, there was an ugly and high fall, with large, pointed rocks underneath.

It was now nearly night, and the hunters thought it was all over with their kind old friend. Sometimes his head would appear, and then his poor old rat-tail would show itself for a moment, when he suddenly raised his head and shoulders from the water, as if to bid them all farewell, and then he went over the fall.

His master wrung his hands in anguish, and several others shed tears as the old friend disappeared, as they supposed, forever.

The hunters gave up the pursuit of the fox, and

returned to their homes with sad faces. Next morning the old campaigner stood at his stable door, in a sad condition, as the night had been cold and he had had no shelter. He was taken to his stable and received the best of care, so in ten days he was as well as ever, and able to take the front rank in the field.

At another time, when The General and his rider were going at a fair rate of speed in Rotten Row, a small boy of the street Arab tribe, unrolled a parcel nearly in front of the horse and his rider, displaying a small, red garment to his admiring, barefooted companions.

As soon as The General saw this fiery piece of dress, which the young Bedouin so suddenly displayed, he made a sudden stand, with a slight retrograde movement. Now it has been affirmed, proved and illustrated by men of science, that when an immovable object is placed unfastened on a movable one, and the movable body suddenly becomes immovable, then the previous immovable body moves on with a greater or less speed, and at a greater or less distance, according to the rate of speed of the movable body at the moment before it becomes immovable. So it was found in the case of The General and his rider, for the latter descended from the back of the former to the face of the earth, which The General would have reached and at the same time, if he had not concluded to halt.

The rider, or he who had been a rider, very soon rose to his feet, and looked as if he saw innumerable stars, and was endeavoring to discover the position of the various constellations. Having finished his observations of the celestial sphere, he turned his eyes to the terrestrial globe, and to the objects animate and inanimate thereon. The first animate thing that he saw was the retreating figure of the descendant of Ishmael, and I may observe here, that it is wonderful how fast a person can run if he has a motive for doing so. The next thing that caught his attention, was his horse, who, contrary to his usual course in such an event, remained perfectly stationary. As he had nothing to run for, he did not run at all.

As may be supposed, this little episode caused a sensation, so that a large number of persons ran to assist the fallen rider; but he assured them that he was not hurt and that he would mount again directly, but that if he could catch that young vagabond, he would teach him not to scare a gentleman's horse.

He had been rather unfortunate in his dress when he was thrown, as one skirt of his coat was torn completely off, having caught in some part of the saddle, and his tall hat, of the style invariably worn by short men, was in a sad condition. Seeing some persons smile, which he thought was for his benefit, he became slightly angry and informed them that he was a plain man, did not care for any one, always paid his way, and rode after the hounds as often as any other man.

Then with the assistance of a policeman and a chair, he mounted his horse and rode from the Park, apparently not very well pleased with his ride.

XVIII.

SELF-MADE MEN.

IN LONDON, as well as in all large cities, there are a large number of rich men who are termed "self-made," who arrived there with only that well known *two and sixpence*. I heard of one who had *three shillings*, but he never became as rich as the others. When they begin to do well and accumulate money, with a good prospect of becoming wealthy, they often speak of their early trials and how they worked and schemed to get a start; but when they have a competence and are perfectly secure, they drop the "two and sixpence," and sink the shop. These men, now being independent, have servants of all grades, fine horses, carriages, and grand mansions, richly furnished.

They endeavor, if not to procure admission to the best, to get admitted into very good society, and generally succeed. Some of them, when they arrive at this stage, discover that they had an ancestor who was a very great man and had some kind of a title, and large estates, who unfortunately took an active part in the wars of York and Lancaster, and lost his property and title at the same time. I have rarely seen a respectable poor person in England, who had not some great and rich ancestor; but by some unfortunate occurrence, or by their intense loyalty to their king, all was lost except honor. These are always very Conservative.

Returning to the self-made man; he intimates sometimes that the title which should belong to him, will some day be restored — which he would accept, even without the estates. He gives those who know him slightly, to think that he could have been elected to the House of Commons, but would not — feeling that his place was among the hereditary legislators. When the names of the members of the Upper House are mentioned, he sometimes appears to have an injured expression of countenance, as if he ought to be where they are.

These persons do no harm. The Government need not be afraid of them. If a Marquis should ever speak to them, it would be *board* for them for several days; but if they were addressed by a Duke, *lodging* must be included.

The wives of these gentlemen, belong to the same

class as their husbands. She who is superior in firmness or intellect, very soon gets the upper hand. If she is not gifted in these qualities, she remains quiet when her lord and master speaks of his great progenitors. When she is his superior, *her* ancestors figure far above *his*, and she wishes to impress this on his mind, on his relatives and friends, and upon her own and his acquaintances.

Her ancestor, as far back as can be traced, was a Montmorency De Spugen, a Frenchman, who lost his title and property during the Huguenot troubles, when he was compelled to fly his country and come to England. The husband's powerful ancestor was a Whitlock Balder, who was always on the right side, if he did lose his title and his property.

Sometimes the husband, in a quiet way, will speak of the Whitlock Balders, and when he is mentioning some event in connection with that illustrious family, the wife will begin with the Montmorency De Spugens, and the poor man immediately subsides into the background. Yet this couple are happy, no doubt, and usually have a son and daughter, who are apparently happy also. They are usually under twenty years of age, well behaved, well educated and well looking, and no doubt will marry well and do well after they are married.

When this quartette are driving in the Park in a splendid carriage, and coachman and footman in dark blue livery, the cortège looks about as well as any other, for the daughter, Miss Anastasia Sophrina, is sure to be very pretty, and most becomingly dressed, while Mr. Percy Constantine, the son, is a very genteel young man, and is said to be doing well at Oxford.

The father looks sideways from his carriage as it goes among the throng. The mother looks straight forward, as if she had always been accustomed to such an equipage. The daughter looks pleasant and pretty, and the son looks a little sad, for he may have some anxiety in regard to Oxford — its rules and his debts there.

XIX.

A TROUBLED LIFE.

SOME persons are fond of relating the history of their lives, particularly when their actions have been as blameless as possible.

A gentleman living in London of middle age who is possessed of a large estate, with fine houses, and with all kinds of property, sometimes relates the history of his troubles in his early years. He has a lovely wife, and a son, who is a fine young man, and now nearly twenty-one years old.

As nearly one-half of this gentleman's life was passed in one locality, I will call the house where he lived, as he names it, the Small House near the corner of the second turning to the right, from the River.

In speaking of himself and others, he says: My earliest life was passed in Paris, where I lived until I was six years old, when I came to England, where I have lived ever since that time.

The mothers of both of my parents died when my father and mother were almost children, and soon after they were dead, my father was sent to Paris to be educated, and my mother to a convent near Paris, where she remained until the time came for her marriage, and she and my father lived in Paris (where I was born) until they left that place for England. My mother's father was an agent for an insurance company, with a good salary, but was extravagant, and when he died, soon after my parents were married, did not leave enough property to pay his debts. But when my mother was in the convent he never allowed her to be in want for anything, for he was determined to make her a lady, and he succeeded.

During my father's school days in Paris, he had learned to speak and write French with fluent accuracy, as also Italian and German, and also to write in these languages. With a knowledge of Latin, and the various branches of mathematics, he had abundance of money, and the fact that he was the only known heir to a large fortune, made him a popular person in Paris. He also had good looks and a good address, and there were few, if any, of the English residents who did not give him a good reception.

The day before we left Paris, my father received a letter stating that his father was dead, with other news of an unpleasant nature. As soon as we could pack our boxes, and pay our bills, we hurried off, and arrived in England in time to attend my grandfather's funeral.

My father had seen little of his father since he had lived in Paris, as his father had only been in that place once since he had ceased to live there, and during that time he had only visited England thrice, each time his visits being short.

Still he had always been attached to his father, and had good reasons for being so, for a more indulgent parent could not be found.

A short time before my grandfather died, it was discovered that there was something wrong about the titles of his estate. I have never known, and I never may know, in what way those titles were wrong, for if there is anything in the world that I hate it is law and litigation.

When we arrived in England we occupied one of father's houses, known as the Small House near the corner of the second turning to the right from the River.

Before we had been in this house a week, we were informed that the estate was in reality not my father's,

— that no part of it, including the house we were occupying was his. Of course my parents and even myself were terribly shocked at this announcement, and I thought my mother would have died after hearing it. It seemed too dreadful to be true, and while my mother was shrieking, and my father endeavoring to pacify her, but weeping like a child at the same time, I was almost bewildered, and, clinging to my mother's dress, asked her " what she was crying for, and what made papa cry; for he never cried before, and I thought he never cried; children and women sometimes cried, but I never saw a man cry before." As I said this, my father caught me in his arms, and said, " Oh, Georgie, you do not know what you have said, or the good that your words have done."

I never again saw my father cry until my mother died, and then I was a young man and did not wonder at his grief.

We continued to occupy the small house which my father was allowed to retain, by paying rent for it.

Then began the struggle for existence, and a very hard struggle it was. My father had a small sum of money left him by his mother, and nearly all of this money found its way into the pockets of Messrs.

Whittler & Grind, lawyers, who had the reputation of being energetic and very sharp. I call these men lawyers, and I call all men the same, who are connected with the law, and by no other name, whether they do or do not wear wigs and gowns, and there is an end of the matter.

My father obtained a few pupils for teaching them French and Italian, and my mother taught music, while I was kept at my books, which were suitable for a child of my age. It was hard work for my parents to live, pay their rent, and supply the wants of Messrs. Whittler & Grind, who were almost continually wanting money, and at the same time making great promises.

My parents' pupils would sometimes fall off. Some would not pay, or their parents would not or could not pay for their instruction. Some were dissatisfied with the instruction. The fact of the matter was that most of the persons with whom we came into contact, knew that my father was a gentleman, and that my mother was a lady, and themselves were neither the one or the other. *There* was where the shoes pinched, and they could not make them easier.

My father had no intimate acquaintances in England, and when his great misfortune overtook him, not one of his former friends in Paris, or those who had since removed to England, or the friends of his father, ever came near him, or wrote to him, and I may say the same in regard to my mother's former friends.

Both of them wrote to their former friends in Paris, but not one of their letters were answered.

I was one day with my mother in Regent street, where she had gone to buy a piece of music, when a lady who had been one of her most intimate acquaintances, (I cannot call her by any other name,) was in her carriage, with a coachman and footman in fine liveries.

She saw my mother, she saw me, and knew us perfectly well, and when I saw her, I said rather loudly, "Oh mamma, there is Mrs. Tompkins in that carriage. There, with the man who has a gilt band on his hat."

Poor little innocent fellow that I was, I thought that Mrs. Tompkins would have the carriage stopped immediately, and insist on our taking a drive with her in Hyde Park, or in some other fashionable place. To my surprise the carriage-lady looked straight forward, merely saying something to the driver, which caused the carriage to move rapidly on.

I asked my mother why Mrs. T. did not speak to her, for I was sure that she saw her. My mother said,

"My dear little Georgie, you are too young for me to tell you why Mrs. Tompkins did not see either you or me." I said, "But she *did* see us. I am sure she did." My mother replied, "Never mind, Georgie, when you are older, you will understand these things."

I was not much older, when I did understand them well — so well that there is not one of those human beings living who insulted or slighted my parents, that I would give a morsel of bread to now, if it was to save them from starvation, and I would not save their necks from the gallows, if I had the power to do so; for of all unpardonable social faults, is the insulting or "cutting" of friends who have by no fault of their own, been brought into difficulties.

We lived and struggled on; sometimes in a state of semi-starvation. Sometimes we had nothing to eat, and almost nothing to wear. Our furniture was nearly all gone, including the piano, and all of our clothes excepting those which we wore, were at the pawn-brokers.

Whittler & Grind said that they must throw up the case if they were not paid for their services, and it seemed almost impossible for my father or my mother to obtain pupils. I would lie in my poor little bed in the corner of the room adjoining that which they occupied, and hear them talk of their troubles, and my name was often mentioned.

I heard my mother say to my father one evening, that if they all lived, Georgie would be a great help to them, as he was nearly nine years old, and very forward for a boy of that age, and that I then could teach French, and was, for a boy of that age, very forward in mathematics, and could also write a beautiful hand. When I heard this, I was determined as soon as possible, not only to earn my living, but also to contribute towards the support of my parents.

Matters with us began to improve a little, and almost enough pupils were obtained to enable us to get our clothes from the pawnbrokers; but the piano was gone beyond redemption, and most of the furniture.

We still retained the small house, although no rent had been paid for a long time, but it was evident that whoever owned or pretended to own it, had reasons for not disturbing us. My father still had hopes of getting back the property, or a part of it, but had no money to pay the lawyers. There was a dissenting clergyman who preached in a small, poor-looking chapel in a narrow street or lane, in a poor locality, not a mile from our house. He was one of the best, if not the very best person that I ever knew. The people who attended his chapel were almost all of them poor. Some were very poor; so the amount of income that he realized was small. This man was almost always busy, and there were few who were sick or destitute, who lived within a mile from his house, that he did not find them and assist them in some way, and he found us, and visited us frequently.

One morning a young man of respectable appearance gave my father a letter, and hurried away.

On opening the same, it was found to contain a ten pound note, and that was all, for the letter was a blank.

This money went to the lawyers. Some more, received shortly after from the parents of our pupils, enabled us to do very well for several months. We went on very much in the usual way for some years, and I was doing my share in teaching, but we were sometimes in a very bad condition. For years, it was the same story, lawyers and all, and bad years were repeated by others.

I had now arrived at the age of nineteen, and was offered a situation with Messrs. Whittler & Grind, as a copying clerk, and to do other little pieces of business, at a salary of sixty pounds a year. Neither my parents nor myself could understand why these men should wish to employ me at such a salary, as I was entirely unacquainted with the business, and any number of young men could be obtained for almost nothing. I accepted the offer, and began my work.

We had paid no rent for our house for a number of years, and no taxes; for we were not called upon to pay either, which was to us a mystery.

After I had been with the lawyers a little over a year, my mother died; and my father never recovered from the grief which her loss gave him, and I never have done so.

I remained with the lawyers until I had passed the age of twenty-one, when I left them.

I was completing some writing in the main office at about ten o'clock one night, when I heard a conversation carried on by my employers, in a small room adjoining, and they evidently supposed that I had gone.

Whittler said to Grind, "His case comes on to-morrow, and you know very well, Grind, that he is sure to gain it, with our evidence, unless "— and here something was said that I could not understand.

"Well, well," said Grind, "if he does gain the case, which he ought to have done, (and you know it,) fifteen years ago, it will be a feather for each of us in our caps; and I am pretty sure that our pockets will receive some additional cash, for we shall have entire control of the estate."

"Right you are," said Whittler, "but how about the boy, for between you and me, I do not think that he has much love for either of us."

"Never you fear about him," said Grind, "I will attend to him, and you know the only reason I had for having him here, was to get control of him and of his father. I will flatter the boy, and also his father, and *we* will manage the property." "Won't he *go* it," cried Whittler, "when he knows about the property?"

"No doubt of it," answered Grind.

I had heard enough, and I left the office as quietly as possible, went home, and told my father what I had heard. He was surprised, and became thoughtful, said little, and soon retired.

That night he had a brain fever, and he died two days after. He was delirious nearly all of the time, and would frequently speak of his absent wife, (sometimes as if she was present,) and of myself. He had been asleep for nearly two hours, and when he awoke he started, saying "Marie, Georgie, my dear boy, I thought I saw her when a cloud — Georgie, (I had taken his hand, and the stout, red-faced doctor was standing near the foot of the bed, crying like a schoolgirl,) — it must be the fog, for I can't see you." His last words (when he screamed like a maniac) were, "I can see it all now — I know it — the fog will not clear away, and I shall never —"

On the day after my father's burial, I was called upon by Mr. Grind; who informed me that I was owner of the small house, and of a large number of large houses. Congratulating me, and receiving very few words in reply, he bowed and retired. In a few weeks my affairs were placed in the hands of an agent who had charge of several large estates, and was a good lawyer. Whittler & Grind were the lowest of the low, for they had played a two-sided game for over fifteen years, and until the old Bachelor false claimant had died, and they were afraid to attempt to squeeze any more from the new party.

The kind clergyman lay on his bed in his modest little room, which was filled with his friends, who knelt before him, some weeping aloud; while he blessed them all, telling them to follow the example of Him who lived in the world over eighteen hundred years ago, and who was poorer than any of them, so poor that he often had no resting place for the night. He was tortured and murdered, after having done all the good that could be done by any one, and after showing people the true way to everlasting life.

Since I have left them, Whittler and Grind have been going down hill, and will continue to descend, until they reach the bottom, where they will remain until they are lowered to their final homes.

I often visit the resting place of my parents, and the flowers covering that place shall never, in their season, wither or decay, during my life. But I can never forgive those who were instrumental in causing to be placed there, these two of my best friends.

Late in the afternoon of a beautiful day in the early autumn, I had gone to this place, and after attending to the flowers, sat down near them, and in looking at one of those beautiful and almost transparent clouds, I fell asleep — but I can never realize that the sleep was a reality.

It seemed as if the cloud was advancing towards me, and when it was almost within speaking distance, it was divided, and there stood those (including the kind clergyman,) whom I had always loved the best, and they all seemed to be looking at me, with looks which are sometimes given by lovely and loved beings, and are never forgotten.

When I awoke, that cloud still appeared in nearly the same position as it was in when I fell asleep, so my sleep must have been short.

The house where my parents' greatest sorrows were known, shall never in any way be altered by me, but it shall still be known as the Small House, near the corner of the second turning to the right, from the River.

XX.

PLACES AND PEOPLE.

IN writing about self-made men, I am reminded of a tale told of the remarkable success of a young man from a very trifling cause, the scene being in London.

It is said that a young man named Lafitte went into a banker's office in Paris, asked for a situation, and was informed by the banker that he had no place for him, and that, as the young man was sadly walking from the office, he saw a pin on the floor, picked it up, and fastened it to his coat.

This act was seen by the banker, who called him back and gave him a situation. The young man did well, became a partner in a few years, and finally one of the wealthiest among European capitalists.

If this tale is a true one, as it is said to be, we may say that the pin is more powerful than the sword, or than some swords.

A tale is told of another young man who went into a banker's office to solicit a situation, and as his references were good, and the banker wanted a clerk, he gave him a situation.

The young man saw a pin on the floor, and as he was fastening it to his coat, the banker told him to leave the house, and never enter it again, for any one who would save a pin in a bank would steal if he had an opportunity for doing so.

Here were two persons who pursued the same course, with entirely contrary results, and we may truly say there is no rule without an exception.

Fortunes are sometimes acquired from acts of unpremeditated kindness, where any good-natured person would have done the same as the successful one.

An old gentleman was walking in Rotten Row, one windy day, when his hat was blown from his head, and went rolling along the road; it seemed very amusing to the large crowd of people, who were not as a class unkind, but a little indiscreet, to see an old gentleman running after his hat, and when he stooped to take it, a gust of wind blowing it still farther. The crowd laughed, but no one attempted to assist the poor old gentleman. Finally, when he was nearly out of breath, a well-dressed, handsome and pleasant-looking young man ran after the hat, caught it, handed it to the old gentleman, and taking him by the arm, kindly led him from the road and to a seat.

The old gentleman thanked the young one for his politeness, and asked him for his card, which was given.

Sometime after this little event, the young man in question received a letter from a solicitor, informing him that he was sole legatee to a large fortune, and I think it is unnecessary to say who was the testator.

It sometimes seems almost useless to follow any course, without deviating slightly from the one followed by others. One commander of a ship follows one course for years, and is always successful, and never meets with the least obstruction. Another takes the same track to the very degree and minute, and encounters an iceberg.

One person builds a yacht which excels all others in speed, and receives an order for another of the same size and shape, of the same material and rigged in the same manner. The first yacht turns out to be a decided success, and the last a decided failure.

One boy at school is quick to learn, fond of sports, and very popular. Another boy, of the same abilities, and his equal in every particular, is disliked by every one in the school, and as he becomes older, is more and more unpopular; — for an unpopular boy will be an unpopular man, and a dull boy at school, who has no taste for either learning or play, will be a dull man, with no taste for business, politics, or rational amusements.

When children are at play, how quick and easy it is to see who among them are naturally bright, and who are stupid. The bright ones are first in all games of fun or mischief, the stupid ones hang back, are always behind, and so continue as long as they live.

Another old gentleman's hat was blown off in the park, and another gentleman of nearly the same age as the one whose hat was blowing away, ran and caught the hat and smilingly handed it to the owner, who, instead of thanking him, said, "Do you think I am such an antediluvian old Egyptian mummy, that I cannot pick up my own hat?" Then the person who had picked up the hat, actually apologized to the old barbarian, for doing him a kindness.

No one rule can always be followed with success; but the rule of honesty and kindness may be followed always, whether we are in a worldly point of view successful or not. A man may defraud another in some way, be what he calls successful, laugh at the man whom he has wronged, and call him a fool. He who cheats or steals is the fool, and the other, if he is honest and just, is the man to be envied. Let these sharpers beware of their tricks, and if they have wronged any one, let them return the entire amount with a good rate of interest, from the time they took what did not belong to them.

When, at last, they are on the beds which they will never leave alive, they will not writhe and cry in agony, which they will do, if they do not make restitution.

Near the northern part of Hyde Park, near the main entrance, is the place where executions formerly took place, before they were done at Newgate, or for crimes committed in the City. This place was called Tyburn, and several squares nearest it are now called Tyburnia.

When crimes were capital, such as sheep-stealing, poaching, shop-lifting and even pocket-picking, there sometimes were several criminals executed at one time.

At Tyburn, Jonathan Wild, Dick Turpin, Jack Sheppard, and a number of other notorious persons are believed to have been executed.

Probably more criminals ended their lives at this

place in the same length of time, than in any other place in the world.

About one mile from Tyburnia, are the new brick barracks, erected for the Horse Guards. Before these buildings were begun, a large number of people were opposed to their being built in or near the Park, as the old buildings which were in the same place, were considered a nuisance, by the people living within a mile or so of them.

The Government wished to have a place to contain soldiers, who could be called out at a moment's notice.

Hyde Park is usually the place where the troubles commence, and a strong body of men well armed, is a good preventive of any sudden outbreak.

Near the west end of the Park, and not far from Kensington Gardens, stands the national monument, erected to the memory of the Prince Consort. It is a handsome structure of the Gothic style, nearly two hundred feet high. The base of granite is about one hundred and fifty feet square. There are at the corners four marble groups, designed to represent the Continents of America, Europe, Asia and Africa. America is represented by a bison of about the usual size of the animal, with a woman on the animal's back, escorted by a man in the backwoods style of dress, and carrying a fire-arm which appears to be a combination of the blunderbuss and an old-fashioned musket. The bison has a very short tail for a bison, and if one of these animals could be seen alive with such a tail, one would almost think that the middle had been cut away, and the two remaining parts brought together and patched up again. This emblematical representation of America, would, to an impartial person, appear to be a failure.

In regard to the groups representing Europe, Asia and Africa, there is a better taste displayed by the artist or the designer. Europe is represented by a handsome bull of the latest approved build, accompanied by a woman, and the other continents are represented by human beings and animals, inhabitants of those countries.

There is a great deal of carving and gilding about the monument, and in the lower part is a gigantic figure of the Prince Consort, completely gilded — the features being very accurate.

XXI.

THE DRAPER'S STORY.

A GENTLEMAN, frequently seen in Rotten Row, quite wealthy, and very popular with his acquaintances, is fond of relating his trials and successes in his younger days, and when he first started in life to make a fortune.

He came from the country, and was a farmer's son, with a very limited education, but had some little knowledge of the business of a draper, having sewed for several weeks in a shop in the country, during the absence of one of the clerks, who was having a few days holiday at the sea-side.

This person had rather more than the usual two and sixpence. He had forty sovereigns, so he was not, for a boy, in a very poor condition in a monetary point of view. He was not entirely unacquainted with London, as he had been in the place several times on business connected with his father's farm, and he had always managed to take care of himself; which sometimes means a great deal; the expression being intended to convey the idea that some other persons are not blessed with the firmness and self-reliance requisite to take care of themselves.

When a person is always boasting of his sharpness, and, to use a common expression, that he has never been taken in, but has frequently taken in others — we had better let him pass by on the other side, or go on the other side when we meet him.

If one of these extra sharp persons should frequent a crowd at the door of any place of amusement, it would be well if attendants of such places had left their valuables at home.

The young countryman could take good care of himself. He was honest and he intended to remain so, if it was possible, but if not, he would return to the country and resume his agricultural pursuits. He had good looks, sound morals and fair abilities. As he was walking in one of the business streets, looking for a place which he thought would suit him, he saw a nice, snug-looking draper's shop, where were sold materials for men's and women's wear, at the lowest possible prices. "Goods sold for cash. Quick sales and small profits. Goods now sold at a great reduction in price, to make room for an overwhelming stock in the coming season. Sales now going on."

Our hero thought that this was the place for him, for there was a live look about the place which reminded him of a country fair or a market, where everything in the way of farm products are disposed of. So he put on a bold face and walked into the shop.

A good-looking, middle-aged gentleman was walking in the main part of the floor between the counters,—this was the proprietor, who asked the stranger what he could do for him, or show him? As the young man had no fear of his being shown to the door, after he had made his business known, with references from clergymen, farmers, and others, he made known his business, and at the same time produced his references.

The draper said that the papers were all right, and as one of his assistants would leave in a few days, a boy would be required to fill his place; the retention of the same, as was always the custom between the employer and employé, being conditional. Then, after adjourning to the counting-house, came the question about terms, or wages.

The draper said that the stranger being the last comer, he would be required to remove the shutters from the windows in the morning, and replace them at night, sweep the shop, carry bundles, collect money, and make himself generally useful.

He was to sleep in the shop, which he was to open in the morning and close at night, his board and washing would be furnished by the concern, and his clothes when he really wanted any, would be furnished also by the concern. After furnishing all of these necessaries, at the close of the year, the further compensation could be considered, and the shop-keeper ended by remarking that he had no doubt whatever of their agreeing about the terms, as the other boys had made the same arrangement, when they first were employed by him.

The countryman knew very well that it would take a tolerably good sized microscope to discover the amount of money that he would receive at the end of the year.

He had hunted foxes, and he knew their tricks pretty well, but he thought that as the fox excelled other animals in cunning, so this gentleman excelled all that he had ever seen in business tact.

He remembered having followed a fox, with a large pack of hounds, in the West of England, when, in coming to a large or high precipice, the fox suddenly disappeared, but the entire pack of dogs went over the rocky precipice, and were nearly all killed. It was discovered that the fox had a secret path in this dangerous place which he had furrowed for the purpose, which led to the disastrous termination of the day's hunt.

At another time, he and several more fox-hunters were close to a fox and the hounds were very near, when the little animal took refuge in a farm-house and went under the bed. The hunters shortly after came to the house and asked permission to enter for the purpose of catching the fox, but were told that, as an Englishman's and an Englishwoman's house was their castle, they could not enter. As for the poor little fox, he had come there for a sanctuary, and should have it. The fox-hunters stormed and threatened, but it was of no use — they were compelled to leave without the fox, who went home to his hole shortly after. It was said that this same fox did the same trick several times.

After the draper had finished speaking of the terms, the countryman told him that he preferred to have a stated salary, and in regard to his board, washing and clothes, he would pay for the necessaries himself, for he might receive considerable money at the end of the year, and he might not, but he considered a bird in the hand to be worth two in the bush, at least, and sometimes more, and if a fox was not certain of being caught and a rabbit was sure of being run down, a person had better give up the fox and stick to the rabbit.

He then returned to the subject of a bird in the hand, and he told the draper that he had a cousin in Canada who was chasing a flock of wild turkeys, when he found a wild goose with a broken wing who could not move as fast as the turkeys, so as he was not sure of the turkeys, but was quite sure of the goose, he secured the latter and let the former go.

The shop-keeper appeared greatly amused by the last story, and asked if geese were plenty in the country where his cousin had settled. The gentleman who is the hero of the tale, says that he could not at that time see why the draper should ask him if geese were plenty in Canada, and say nothing about turkeys, for turkeys were well known to be much finer birds.

The young man finally named a stated amount of salary for the year, and declared that he would not take a farthing less, which was in a few minutes' time accepted by the shop-keeper, who now began to read him a lecture on economy, and endeavored to show to him that the less a clerk received the more he would save, and mentioned a young man who saved more when he received fifty sovereigns a year than he did when his salary was raised to one hundred.

The draper further said that boys should be saving, and the sophist would probably, if he had continued his lecture on economy much longer, have endeavored to prove that a boy would save more money without a salary than he would with one. It seemed to the countryman that the draper mentioned the word boys rather often, considering that all of his employés were full grown men, and he, the countryman, was nearly twenty-one years of age.

He finally gave the draper to understand that, although he had lived in the country, and was used to green things, he himself had somewhat ripened. He entered upon his duties. The draper and he were on the best of terms, the business was increased, and finally he became a partner, and in the course of time, a rich man. He retired several years ago with a comfortable fortune.

This gentleman was not afraid to work when he was a boy, for he was always ready to do anything that the draper required, and when the latter saw what a good, straightforward fellow he was, and that he could do more work of every kind than any other two of his clerks, from packing goods to selling them, the young man was, as a matter of course, promoted, and the rest followed in due course.

It is frequently the rule in London that the rich business men begin a business life in a very humble way, and a good part of them came from the country, some being farmers' sons.

These young men come to the City with the intention of remaining, and when they are fortunate enough to obtain a situation, they intend to retain the same. Besides, they know that the hardest work in a shop of any kind, is easy compared to the work they do on a farm. They wear better clothes in the city than in the country, and when they have been in the city for a short time, if they have good principles, consider themselves men.

In the Park when the roads and walks are not much frequented by the better classes, the vagrants and those who are out of work, assemble every pleasant day, (or when the weather is not cold enough to be compelled to remain within doors) and sit on the benches or lie on the grass.

There are not so many of this class in Hyde Park as

there are in the other parks, including St. James's, Green, Regent's, Victoria, Battersea, Primrose Hill and Kensington Gardens. All of these are large, with lakes on a small scale, trees, shrubs, beautiful flowers, and plenty of ground covered with grass.

Large spaces of ground are used for cricket playing, for military parades, and for meetings of various kinds.

All of the lakes have boats, which may be used by any one paying for the same, and these lakes have water-fowl, including swans.

Hyde Park is the only one where riding or driving is indulged in. The gates of these parks are closed at a certain hour at night, and all persons who are then seen by the police are compelled to withdraw.

They sometimes contrive to conceal themselves in the shrubbery or under the benches, and continue in concealment during the night.

These vagrants are composed of persons who work a little, who beg a little, but steal a great deal if they have an opportunity of doing so.

Burglars and more daring thieves are said by the detectives to despise these vagrants and petty thieves, and all of those who sit and lie in the parks.

Sometimes one of these vagabonds who is more

THE DRAPER'S STORY. 141

ambitious than the others of his class, procures a broom and embarks into business, and into a sea of mud and troubles. If some of them had considered the uncertain, annoying, dangerous and unhealthy business in which they had invested their capital, and which required their utmost talents and energies to prosecute successfully, they would have either remained out of active business or have used their talents, capital and energies in some other line of business.

They might have become solicitors (or *cads*) for cabmen, which profession is popular among the classes who are found near the standing places for cabs and hansoms. The duties of such persons are to find a cab or hansom for any one who wishes to enter one of these vehicles, and to open and close the doors, receiving usually the sum of one or two-pence for their services.

When most persons embark in business, they think that they do so with their eyes open, and should any one volunteer their advice, they are given to understand that the embryo business person knows what he or she is about, and when they want advice they will ask for it.

The persons who do not wish for advice from any

one, are sometimes right and sometimes wrong, according to circumstances.

The advice of a person sometimes may not be good, and then if it is good, it may not be followed; so in either case the adviser is placed in an unpleasant position. Unless persons are responsible for the success of their children or those who are entrusted to their care, perhaps it will be better to give no advice, or no voluntary advice.

When any person of the vagrant or of the semi-vagrant class, are in any way personally deformed, their fortune (according to the ideas of a fortune of that class) is made, and the greater the deformity the greater the fortune, for the most persons pity these creatures and give them money.

Some few of these vagrant and semi-vagrants are honest; more of them are honest probably than is generally supposed. But their habits are such that as a class they are regarded with suspicion.

A man was arrested two or three years ago for begging, who was by profession, a street-crossing sweeper, and who had been known to receive more than a sovereign a day for his professional services. He was asked by the magistrate why he had been begging. He answered that owing to the long period of dry weather, his business had fallen off, and as he had lived up to his income during his time of prosperity, he had nothing left when hard times came, and was compelled to ask for assistance. But he added, if the persons who advanced him money would call at his residence when business improved, he would repay them.

He also said that when business revived and money was more plenty, his business would be conducted in a better way, and that he would endeavor to increase his capital, and live within his income, so that he would be able to meet all liabilities in unprosperous times. He was discharged with a caution, resumed business, and the weather having been rainy the greater part of the time for two years, has been very successful.

A butcher who is doing a good business, says that a street-sweeper always buys the best of meat, and that they generally have plenty of money.

When one street-crossing sweeper encroaches on the domain of another, there is trouble, and if he cannot be expelled by one, several will assist in doing so, and he is banished from the fraternity. When one of them retires from business, if he is a man of family, his son or daughter continues the business, or sometimes his wife or widow does so. The street-sweeping is often sold for a large sum.

It is unnecessary to say that the vagrant and semi-vagrant class in England are very ignorant, and neither they nor their ancestors ever knew the benefits of the common education, and the greater part of them would, if it were not for the laws, punish their children for attending school.

The boot-blacking business is conducted here in the same way as in American cities.

The boys who sell newspapers are better dressed and better behaved than those who are engaged in the same business in America, but the American boys are much sharper. The dealers in small articles of merchandise, which is usually carried in baskets, are about the same kind of persons as are seen in America.

There appear to be different grades of society among the people of humble pursuits, as well as among those of higher grades.

Some time ago a young *boot-black* married the daughter of a street-crossing sweeper, greatly to the annoyance and mortification of the parents of the boot-black, who had designed their son for a person of a higher position. The girl whom their son had married had not been accustomed to move in the same circles as they or their son had moved in, and they feared that their son's wife, by her manners in society, would place her husband and themselves in an unpleasant situation. In fact, the bride's conduct was not entirely exemplary during the wedding tour, which extended from the Charing Cross landing to Greenwich and back.

A few years ago the son of a groom married the daughter of a coachman. Both the groom and coachman were employed in the same family. There was a terrible commotion in the coachman's family when it was known that the wedding had taken place; for they all exclaimed that the girl had lowered herself and them, by uniting herself with a common groom. The coachman had been accustomed to associate with other coachmen of high positions.

Some of them actually powdered their hair, and one of them was with a person of title. The coachman said his daughter could have done much better, for there was young Jeames Tapen, the rich draper's son, had taken Hagnes Jane to the Hadelphi, and now she had gone and done this. Oh, oh dear, what should they do. The gentleman who employed the coachman and the groom, was a kind man, and when he saw the state of affairs, he promoted the groom in some way, and the coachman's family were finally reconciled.

About five years ago a cook, fifty years old, brought an action against a coachman for breach of promise of marriage. The correspondence between the lovers caused some sensation in the Court during the trial. The jury gave the plaintiff one hundred and fifty pounds damages.

The juries usually give damages in favor of the plaintiff in these actions, and they seem to know the amount of the defendant's capital, and then take it all.

About two years ago a gentleman brought an action against a lady for a breach of promise, but gained nothing, either in a monetary or in a social sense, excepting notoriety.

If this is the way the male sex are to be treated, the fair sex should make the proposals, and then a jury may view an action in a breach of promise affair, by a new and improved light.

XXII.

HOW AN M. P. GETS ON.

THE Clergymen in England of all sects are esteemed as much as in America, and wherever they go, and whatever position they are placed in, are invariably respected, and great deference is shown them by all classes, with scarcely any exception. A large majority of these gentlemen receive small salaries, and, when they have families, sometimes find it difficult to support them, and also to assist the poor — which they very often do. They visit the sick and the destitute, and there are but few places that have not seen the faces of these kind gentlemen.

They have one advantage over a great many others, for they can educate their children in every point of view, and if the children of clergymen mistake the right path for the left one, they certainly are exceptions to the generality of clergymen's children, who generally do well.

Most of these gentlemen have no sure prospect of improving their worldly condition, but sometimes by the resignation or death of those few who were in better conditions in a pecuniary way, they fall into their places, and then after a long time of work, they are allowed a little repose.

* * * * * *

Most of the Members of Parliament visit the Park every fine day during the Parliamentary season, which they can do, as the business hours of both houses is in the afternoon.

If a Member of Parliament is not popular, or I should say not interesting, he is not listened to, and the members appear to have suddenly caught severe colds; they groan and cough as if they were in pain, and by the noises they make with their feet, it would seem to a person who is not familiar with Parliamentary proceedings, that quite a number had the St. Vitus dance, or were practising some other dance.

While I think of it — would it not be a good change in the rules of Parliament, during the business hours, if the members would remove their hats from their heads? In all other meetings held within doors, all persons remove their hats on entering the room, and as Parliamentary meetings are the first in the country, the members surely ought to do the same.

It is well for every country to be to a certain extent conventional, and to adhere to old customs, and to be adverse to sudden radical changes. But in sailing down the river of Time, the main course of the stream may become changed, and it will be necessary to find new channels to avoid obstructions.

When these members have succeeded in demolishing the new or unpopular member, and they are pretty sure that he will not continue much longer, some of them leave the room, and make considerable noise in doing so.

The poor Member who is trying to make himself heard, after first looking indignant, speaking louder, stammering and blushing, generally is compelled to give it up and sit down, with a look, and evidently with a feeling of shame, disappointment and chagrin, that no one but himself, can have the most remote idea of; and no one can realize what were the feelings of that poor disappointed, would-be orator, unless he has been placed in the same situation. Sometimes a member who has failed, or who has been put down by the others, makes another trial, and, by holding his ground, does succeed, in spite of his tormentors. Most of them are backward in making the second attempt

Sometimes a member who has risen to make his first speech, and the other members will not hear him, leaves the room foiled, but not conquered. He has failed in his first speech — that speech which he had prepared before with so much care, and which he had rehearsed again and again, until every word was as familiar to him as the first three letters of the alphabet, and when delivered in his semi-theatrical voice, which would electrify the house — has been a complete failure.

As he turns to leave the House, he cannot avoid looking at those men, sitting and standing, with looks of pleasure and satisfaction, at his discomfiture, some looking at him and then nudging their companions and laughing at the same time.

He saw all this, and he never forgot it. He went home and to his room, and threw himself into a chair. If he had been a woman, he would have cried as if his heart would break; but he was a man, and others had failed and their hearts were not broken, and in the end they succeeded, and why should he not succeed?

He will go to the House regularly, attend to his duties, and try to give satisfaction to his country, his constituents and himself.

These reflections are beneficial to him. Hereafter he is always in his seat and ready to cast his vote at the proper time, is very attentive to the rules of the house, and has made up his mind never to annoy men who are speaking, but to cheer them or be quiet.

This member endeavors to be on good terms with every one, and very soon succeeds in having a number of friends representing both parties; always listening with great attention to the remarks and suggestions of every member that he comes in contact with. When a man on his own side of the house makes a speech, he is as willing as any one to cry, "hear, hear;" but will, in a mild way, express his disapprobation of some of the speeches on the other side.

He now gives some nice dinners, and he invites those who he is sure will be, at some time, of service to him. They all come — some of them being the very men who annoyed him when he attempted his first speech, and who were mainly instrumental in his failure. He knows these men perfectly well, but they think he did not notice them on that unpleasant occasion. The dinner passes off very well; but during the same, the host asks a question of the most rising member, and he is answered very soon, and then the

HOW AN M. P. GETS ON.

host makes a remark which leads to a slight discussion, when the giver of the dinner makes such well-timed and sensible remarks, without giving the least offence to any one, that the guests are surprised, and almost delighted.

A short time after the dinner, he ventures to make a short speech in the House, and is heard with decided success.

His speeches in Parliament become longer than they were when he was first allowed to deliver them. He is heard with great attention by both parties, and remembers well that day when he made his first attempt, and a few hours after, his age had seemed to have increased by as many years as the number of hours. During his parliamentary career, he may be called upon to fill a high position — perhaps the highest in the kingdom.

Thus, in the course of time, this successful man has reached the summit of the hill of life; but the summit of the hill of ambition he cannot attain, and is compelled to descend to his future home. The descent is easily made, for the path is straight, and there are no obstructions. But when he is near his home, as the shades of night are approaching, he casts a last, long, lingering look at that hill whose summit no one ever reached, and then with a sad but resigned expression, resumes his compulsory tour. He soon arrives at the place, where there are no hills to descend; but, on every side, a broad plain of eternal peace.

Aide toi, et le ciel t'aidera.

XXIII.

GENTLEMEN OF THE BAR.

THE JUDGES of the various Courts in England are selected for their abilities and for their honesty, which is above suspicion. The summing up of some of them appears like the addresses of our prosecuting attorneys. They are undoubtedly right. They are sustained by the Government, and a person is never, or very seldom, wrongfully convicted.

The salaries of some of the Judges are larger than any American official receives, who is connected with the Government, excepting the President, and they hold their positions for life, or until they retire, when they are liberally pensioned.

Promotion from a lower to a higher Court frequently occurs, owing to the resignation or death of those of the higher grades.

The Judges, and other men of the higher branches of the profession, wear white horse-hair wigs, and gowns, when they are in court; but the inferior grades, such as attorneys and solicitors, appear in plain dress.

Some of this lower grade are never enabled to obtain much business. But to hear some of them conversing with those of their own class, a stranger who is unacquainted with the mysteries of the profession, would naturally suppose that they had more work in the courts than they were able to attend to. Sometimes they speak quite loud and have rather a pompous look, and sometimes they have been known to say to their equals or their slightly superiors, that Mr.—— (mentioning the person's name of course,) who is a banker's clerk, "is a very good sort of fellow, but *we* of the profession, you know, cannot associate with him on equal terms, you see."

When two of these persons are in a restaurant, or some place where they are not very well known, and where many are present, one or both of them will take a large envelope from one of their pockets, the same having a decided legal appearance.

These small gentry generally dress rather smartly, and their coats are always a little longer or shorter than the prevailing style. When these persons meet those who are above them in the same business, they say very little, but seem to listen very attentively, always agreeing with their superiors. When they meet with those just one grade above them, they say in reply to some remark made by the superior legal light, "Yes, yes. Quite true. I made the same remark to Green, the other day, and he agreed with me, and wondered that he had not seen it before." When they come into contact with a new light who is just entering, intending at some time to electrify all other lights, then these semi-subordinates are in the very pinnacle of their glory. They are able to give the new comer every information, not only in regard to law but in many other things. They are perfectly familiar with Coke, Blackstone and Starkie, and are always ready to give an opinion or advice, whether either of them is solicited or not, and for some days the novice is greatly impressed with their immense knowledge.

One of these small lawyers who was in the company of his friends, remarked to them that he had lately recovered some property for his Lordship, (mentioning the title,) and he had at the same time given some advice to his Lordship, and for so doing, he had received his Lordship's thanks, with an assurance from his Lordship, that if his Lordship should ever again require his services, his Lordship would employ him, Mr. Splutter.

"His Lordship" lived in the country a short distance from London, and had a number of fine horses, among them one who was a favorite hunter.

Toby Dingle, the groom, had charge of a few of the horses, among them was this favorite hunter who was called Jack. One evening, Mr. Dingle asked his master if he could go to meet some friends at a farm-house about five miles distant, and if he might ride Jack. His Lordship, a kind man, readily gave the permission.

Dingle enjoyed the visit, returning at two o'clock on the following morning, and having placed Jack in the stable, retired to his room above.

His Lordship was an early riser, and this morning visited his stables, and the gate leading to the stables, and the stable door leading to Jack's stable were both open, and his favorite hunter gone. He immediately went to Toby Dingle's room, and told him to get up, for the door was open and Jack was gone. It did not take long for Dingle to complete his toilet, for he had omitted to remove his clothes, including his boots.

"Well, Toby," said his master, "what do you think of this? It is a bad affair."

"Well, your Lordship," said Dingle, "I think 'ow

some thief has stolen that horse, for I have the key in my pocket, and the vagabond must have picked the lock." His Lordship had his own opinion, but said nothing, and it was not necessary at that time to do so, as the horse made his appearance in the company of Mr. Splutter, the young lawyer, who had been in the country a short distance, to spend the day, and had left his entertainers early in the morning, to be in time for business. He had not gone far before he saw his Lordship's horse, saddled and bridled, entertaining himself by eating grass on the side of the road.

Mr. Splutter knew the horse at once, and the horse knew him, for Splutter had ridden him in Rotten Row by the permission of his Lordship, for the latter, who had a kind feeling for the young lawyer, on account of his father, who had once been in his employ, and was always a good and faithful servant.

His Lordship thanked his young friend for the restoration of the horse and gave him two sovereigns, which was probably the first fee that Mr. Splutter had received since he had been admitted as an attorney. This was the true account of the recovery of the property.

XXIV.

VICISSITUDES OF FASHION.

THE ladies in London and also in New York and the other American cities dress so much in the same style, that it is difficult on seeing them in the Park or in any of the streets of London, to decide who are Americans and who are English. The fashions change here as often as they do in New York and Paris, indeed, a little too often for the benefit of the generality of the people.

Why people in Europe and America should be in favor of changing the fashions so often is a mystery, when they know perfectly well that these continual changes are made by the milliners and dress-makers to increase their own business and profits. These certainly cannot be blamed, for doing as well as possible, no more than people who are engaged in other kinds of business, but, when an article of dress is as good at the end of a year as it was at the beginning, it would seem as extravagant to throw it aside, as it would to throw aside a carpet, or any furniture purchased at the same time as the article of dress.

History is said to repeat itself, and the same may be said in regard to fashions; for some of the fashions for ladies' bonnets at the present time are the same, (if the old fashion plates are correct,) as those of one hundred or more years ago. If the fashions are good, why change them? and then go back to the old style.

A Government may require a change to suit the times, but it would seem to be useless to make the change and then in a few years go back to the old form, for all of this trouble would be a waste of time; and besides the new ideas formed by the change would be creeping up and agitating the people.

The fashions are seldom changed in Spain, yet there is not a prettier or more becoming dress in the world than that of the Spanish ladies.

These continual changes are expensive, and ruinous to some, and if ladies would adopt some becoming style, like the Spanish ladies, and adhere to it, they would appear a great deal better, and they would at the same time to a certain extent be public benefactors.

In regard to the dress of gentlemen it is difficult to discover any change for the last twenty years or more, or not change enough for a gentleman to be ashamed of a coat made twenty years ago, if the same is good and did not show by its being threadbare, that its owner was a miser or misanthropist.

When we go to an opera or a theatre and see people, who by their dress and manners portray the same of the people of one or two hundred years ago, we come away perfectly charmed, and think the style of Louis XIV. very pretty and becoming, and for one change of fashion in those days, there are twenty now.

Yet after writing this, I must say that I do like to see persons well dressed, and when they are not well attired they are disagreeable.

All ladies may continue the fashions of the present time for years, and at the same time be well dressed.

XXV.

JOHN CUFF AND THE SEAL.

THE Serpentine River (or canal), by the permission of the Government, is used by the people for a bathing place in the summer. Those who bathe in it are restricted as to the time, which is in the evening, or after the visitors leave the Park.

Among the good swimmers is a man of about thirty years of age, one Joseph Cuff, who by his feats in swimming, attracts more than usual attention.

He lives in a small town not far from London, at least not far for these times of rapid traveling.

This person has never been engaged in any regular occupation, but is always ready to do anything that he can, with or without pay.

He loses nothing by his willingness to oblige, for he picks up a good many shillings in the course of a year, and receives a large number of good dinners from people who are his friends and patrons. He is well known for miles around the town where he lives, and every one is his friend. He will carry children across the streets when the latter are muddy, and he will take orders to butchers, drapers, or any tradesmen for families in the town, and everything that he does he does well, and gives entire satisfaction.

People would call to him as he passed by and ask him if he would be so kind as to go somewhere and do something, and he would cheerfully do as he was asked.

He had often been offered good situations, but would never accept of them, for he preferred being his own master. His usual dress was an entire corduroy suit, with a seal-skin cap. He wore this dress in doing rough work, but had better clothes for other kinds of occupations, such as were wanted for waiting at the table, and driving a gentleman's carriage, etc. On Sunday he regularly attended the small chapel, dressed in a good suit of black, and was always attentive to the sermon.

When the pastor saw Cuff, he always spoke to him, and the invariable answer was, "I hope your Reverence is quite well," raising his hat at the time.

Mr. Cuff was at every wedding, ball or social assembly of every kind that had been held in the town for fifteen years, always holding some position where he could see every person, and could probably give a better account of the proceedings than any other person.

Cuff really seemed to enjoy life, which is more than a great many others do, who have the apparent luxuries of life.

This good, honest, simple man was making a short visit to London, and was amusing himself and others in the Serpentine, by diving and remaining under the water longer than any other person, walking the water with his head and shoulders above the same, and then showing his feet above, his head being under the water at the same time. The other bathers were delighted and Cuff received many cheers and congratulations, for entertaining them.

A showman three or four years ago, was going towards London with a large Arctic seal in a covered wagon. As he came to a lake on the outskirts of the town where Mr. Cuff lived, he concluded to give his seal a bath. He had a leather harness on the animal, with a long rope tied to it, so he could pull the animal ashore when he wished him to resume his journey. About the time that he had drawn the seal into the water, the rope broke or became separated from the harness, and the seal was loose, and appeared to enjoy his liberty. He jumped a number of feet from the water, standing on his head and on his tail, rolling over and swimming on his back and on his sides, and then dived, disappearing for nearly one-half of a minute, reappearing a hundred yards or more further from the shore. Nothing would induce him to come to his master or to pay the least attention to him, for he seemed determined to enjoy himself while he had the opportunity.

The people assembled to see the seal and to enjoy his pranks, and his master's trouble. A boat was procured, and the showman, with three men rowed towards the seal with the intention of capturing him, by fastening fish to ropes, so when the seal swallowed the fish, he could be drawn to the boat and secured.

The animal was too knowing for them. He looked at the fish when they were first displayed, as if he would like them very well, but was afraid of the ropes, and was pretty sure that they were to be used in some way to entangle him. Perhaps he had already partaken of a few fish from the lake, and knew that he could have some more when he wanted them.

After the men in the boat had rowed around the

animal for some time, and could do nothing for the owner of the seal, they concluded to row to the shore and hold a consultation.

Mr. Cuff had by this time arrived, and when the boat touched the shore, stepped forward and said to the proprietor of the seal, " I beg pardon, Master, but I think I can catch that beast, if I may do it in my own way."

The showman, after being informed of the name of the person who volunteered his services to recover his live property, answered, "Well, Mr. Cuff, if you can do so, you will do me a great favor, and receive ten shillings for your services."

A rope was given to Cuff and he made a noose, similar to those used in South America for catching wild cattle. He then removed his coat and boots, retaining his other clothes, for he said that the creature might attempt to bite him, and his corduroys, woolen stockings and cap would be a protection, and he would take good care of his face and hands. By this time the greater part of the population of the town were on the border of the lake looking at Cuff and the seal.

Cuff declared his intention of swimming to the seal, throwing the noose over him, and towing him ashore, for he said the animal could be caught in no other way, as he was afraid of the boats and the men in them. If the seal saw him with his old seal-skin cap, in the water, he would not slip away, but stop and look at the new object in the water, and then the noose could be thrown over his head, and the animal secured and towed to the land, and replaced in the wagon.

The owner of the seal cautioned Cuff to be on his guard, as the animal might attempt to seize him, and if he was successful, could dive, and remain under the water long enough to drown him.

He also told Cuff that these animals would bite as savagely as any ferocious dog, and warned him to care for himself, to put on a bold front, for seals were naturally cowardly, and would generally retreat, if their adversaries were bold, and came directly towards them.

Cuff said that he was not afraid of any amphibeous animal, for he could stay under water as long as any of them, and he could drown some of them. Nor was he afraid of the creature's teeth, for Bill Jinks had a big bull dog, who had tried to bite through his corduroys when he took the beef from the dog that the latter had grabbed from Tilda as she was preparing it for dinner. That dog tugged away at them, and would not let go until he was choked off. The dog had left the marks of his teeth on them, but they were not injured.

About this time the seal, which was more like a sea lion than a seal, came near the shore, pitching and diving about, and looking rather more formidable than Mr. Cuff supposed a seal could look.

Cuff had a good view of the animal, and seemed to be a little nervous, but had gone too far to retreat with honor. Besides, all or nearly all of his companions were present, with a large number of friends of the better classes, and if he should now back out, he would be disgraced for ever.

He wound the rope around his waist, leaving several yards loose.

Now he was ready, and jumping into the water, swam towards the place where he had last seen the seal. When he arrived there, the seal made his appearance, about ten yards in his front, and when the animal saw the fur cap, and the shoulders and arms of the swimmer, he remained motionless, and seemed surprised, as if he hardly knew what to do, whether to advance or retreat. Cuff was evidently afraid of the seal, which he thought was about to attack him. So he went under the water, and the seal disappeared at the same time. When the latter arose to the surface, Cuff was on his back, and slipped the noose over the head, and around the body of the seal, which would not slip from it, as the harness which it still wore kept the rope in its place, and held very firm, the noose being drawn very tight by Mr. Cuff. The seal now made another dive, carrying Cuff along with him, and when they arose, the rider looked a little careworn and fatigued.

The seal now commenced a series of extraordinary motions, such as swimming very fast, turning suddenly around, trying to jump from the water, and so on, but not being able to do so with Cuff on his back, would make a dive, and then dart through the water near the surface, invisible himself, but allowing Cuff's head to appear just above the water. Cuff afterwards said that he wished that he could have had a pair of spurs on his heels at that time, for he would have made the aggravating creature tired of his manœuvres. Cuff still clung to the seal, and when the animal last appeared, his rider pulled off his old fur cap, and placed it over the eyes and head of the creature, who stopped, surprised and bewildered, and remained perfectly still, when a boat containing the animal's owner and three others, came near, and the rope was caught, and Cuff and the seal were pulled into the boat, the first being taken on board, and the latter towed to the shore, and placed in the wagon.

Mr. Cuff received a sovereign instead of ten shillings from the showman, and the people of the town gave him enough shillings to amount to several sovereigns. So this piece of work was the most profitable one that he had ever accomplished.

After this episode in the life of Mr. Cuff, he was more popular than ever. If a serious accident had occurred to him in capturing the seal, it would have gone hard with the seal and its owner. When Cuff was in his dangerous situation, the people began to look rather dark at the showman, and some said that he ought to be in Cuff's place. Others said that they wished the seal and his owner were where the seal first came from.

XXVI.

THE CONFIDENTIAL CLERK.

HISTORIANS, not being always accurate, differ (like common mortals,) in their accounts of governments, and the people in them, also in their accounts of battles, sieges, retreats, etc. One historian writes of a battle where one army obtains a great victory, and the other army is badly defeated and retreats, leaving an overwhelming number of dead, wounded and prisoners behind them. Another historian, in giving his account of the same affair, says that the so-called defeated army moved on for strategic purposes, in order to gain a good position, so that they could demolish the enemy when the opportunity for doing so arrived. Impartial persons may say that the army that moves on, sometimes move at a considerable distance, before they are satisfied with the position, and then when they find a good place for annihilating the enemy, something occurs to cause them to move on again, and they never seem to find a good strategic position, until they reach their homes, or headquarters.

If the historians in our time are not accurate, with the means at their command for being so, surely the old and ancient historians are not to be entirely relied upon, when they speak of millions of men in one army, and of an overwhelming number, (large enough to conquer an ordinary kingdom,) being defeated by a comparatively few soldiers, who are not enough in numbers to constitute half of a fair sized regiment in our time.

One person writes a biography wherein the individual is described as almost a fiend, and if that person is a woman, that she has been guilty of horrible crimes, and if she holds a high and strong position in the government where she lives, that no one is safe within that government.

Another biographer will describe her as being kind and charitable, just and pious.

Some will describe a king as a perfect monster of iniquity, guilty of the worst of crimes; but in the course of time, some one else will write a more favorable account of this supposed monster, and when some persons reflect on the subject, they think that there might have been some good qualities in the character of the firm and unforgiving king, after all that had been written to the contrary.

We are not compelled to believe a person who relates to us the history of his own life; but, if we write his biography, we should accept his statement, and leave inventions for another biography, or history.

A gentleman in giving an account of the place where the most exciting part of his life was passed, said, "I was the confidential clerk in the old established warehouse, near the Docks.

"I have a recollection, when I was a child, five years old, of living in London, in a good house, which was occupied by a gentlemen and his wife, with two female servants. The entire party were kind and honest people and I was always treated well by every one of them. I think that all of them are now living, as I have seen them quite recently. I was sent to a school in London, where I received a fair education; but during that time I lived with this family, and when I was sixteen years of age, I was placed by the gentleman, (with whom I had lived as long as I remembered having lived anywhere,) in the old established warehouse, near the Docks.

"From the age of five to sixteen, I had known nothing of my parents, and remained entirely ignorant on that subject until I had passed the age of twenty, when my father made himself known to me.

"The proprietor of the warehouse was over fifty, and the house and the business had been owned by his father and grandfather.

"He was a fine man, with splendid business qualifications, and very wealthy for a person in that line of business. He was married and had one child, a daughter of nearly my age, who was at that time at a convent in France, where she was educated.

"From the age of five to ten years, I had frequently inquired of my friends if they knew any thing of my father or mother, for other children had fathers and mothers, and I supposed that I was entitled to the same blessings. My guardian finally told me that I would never see my father or mother, and he hoped that I would never speak or ask any more questions about them.

"I cried bitterly, but my protector placed me on his knee, and told me that I ought not to cry. I thought that his voice seemed strange, or entirely different from its usual sound, while his wife was weeping as if her heart would break. He then told me that I should think of other boys who had no parents, and were poor and miserable, without homes and without friends, and some children had bad fathers and mothers, who drank whiskey and gin, beat their children, and starved them. This pacified me, and I said no more about my parents.

"When I went to the warehouse, I was employed as an assistant book-keeper, but in two years was the cashier, and held that position until I became a partner in the concern. There was, among the proprietor's employés, a young man who was in the house when I was employed, who had been there for about one year, and from the first day of my arrival, we had a mutual dislike for each other. He was about twenty-five years of age, rather tall, with black hair and cats' eyes — the latter were unlike the eyes of a human being, and different from any that I have ever seen. He was very active, and sometimes rather noisy, but had considerable ability, and was considered to be a valuable clerk. He did a part of the out-of-doors work, and did it well, but I never liked or trusted him, and I very rarely spoke to him, or he to me, unless the affairs of the concern compelled us to do so. After I had been promoted to the position of cashier, the proprietor's daughter came home, having finished her education, and one day she and her mother came in a carriage to the warehouse.

"I had never seen such a lovely girl as this, and she was apparently as accomplished, sensible and good, as she was beautiful. The fact of the matter was, I was at first sight in love with her, and she knew that such was the fact, but whether her mother, who introduced us, was at that time aware of it, I am unable to determine.

"The clerk with the black hair was also introduced to the young lady, and in a moment I saw the impression that she had made upon him, and I can assure you that the previous impression that he had made upon me, was not removed by that which the young lady had made upon him.

"She looked at him with a look of wonder, and I am sure that from that day she never spoke to him, and only gave a slight nod to him when she visited the warehouse.

"I had been accustomed to place in a drawer of the writing desk a little money, amounting to thirty pounds, for paying small sums during the day, and the money consisted of sovereigns, half sovereigns, silver and copper.

"There was a young man or boy in the warehouse, about seventeen years of age, who attended to a portion of the out-of-doors work, and who was liked by every one in the house, even by the cat-eyed man, if he could like any one but the fair daughter of the proprietor. One day I went to lunch, and forgot to lock the cash drawer in my desk, and when I returned, the cat-eyed man and the boy were in front of the desk, not very far from it. I saw that the boy was pale and agitated, but the man was humming an opera air.

"The boy appeared anxious to speak to me, but seemed afraid to do so until the other went away. I thought there was something wrong with that desk, and never left it for a moment that afternoon, until the house was closed. The boy was sent out of the house to attend to some business, and the man was inside nearly the entire afternoon. I saw that he kept near the desk, and I knew then very well that he wanted to slip some money into that drawer, that he had taken out of it when I had gone for my lunch. During the afternoon he stooped down, and among the pieces of torn paper under the desk and under the cash drawer, he caught up a piece of paper which he had evidently dropped, at the same time exclaiming, 'There, I have found it finally, and how it came there I can't tell,' and he began his opera tune again, and went about half way down the room. The boy's work kept him away, and he did not return when the house was closed, and I saw him no more alive. When I counted the cash that evening, there were two sovereigns short. The man with the green eyes was not far off, and I said that the cash was short two sovereigns, when he looked at me with those animal eyes, and shortly said, 'Well, that is strange, are you sure that you have counted it right?' 'Quite sure,' said I, for I thought that I had him fast.

"I was mistaken. He said: 'That old rickety desk and drawer are not fit for money or any thing else. I shouldn't be surprised if the money had dropped on the floor in some way; and you know when you are paying the little bills, and a number of men around, you very often have a heap of sovereigns and silver on the top of that old desk, which slopes down more than any I ever saw, and I have often wondered at your not dropping the whole lot of gold and every thing else, among the rubbish on the floor.' This he spoke rather sharply.

"What he said was true, and I did at one time drop the greater part of the contents of the drawer on the floor, and had some trouble in finding it all again. While I was considering this matter, and thinking that I would be more careful, this man said: 'There they are, as I supposed, among the papers,' and he gave me a contemptuous look and walked down the room.

"I had agreed to meet a friend that evening, to accompany him to the theatre, and as soon as I had locked the safe, I hurried away to eat my dinner and meet my friend.

"The next morning, the boy, who was out all the afternoon, was found dead in his bed, without the least marks of violence, although his features were distorted. An inquest was held, and it was found that he had died from some cause unknown, a post-mortem examination having taken place previously.

"This fellow clerk who found the money, was too much for me in some things. He was present at the inquest and funeral, and as composed as I ever saw him. The proprietor, his wife and daughter, and all the employés, were greatly shocked and grieved at the death of the nice little fellow, for he was a favorite with all of them. I say nothing about the mean rascal, when I speak of this grief.

"I had passed the age of nineteen and for some time

had (at the invitation of my employer,) visited his house, where I was always well received by the daughter and her mother, and intended to make known my wishes in regard to the daughter when I was twenty years old. The father told me one day that if I never knew my parents, he knew very well that my father was considerably above the middle classes. He said that he was informed of the fact by his friend, the gentleman who procured me the situation, and that was enough for him to know.

"I asked him if he knew anything about my mother, and he said that he only knew that my father and mother were married in a small town in Scotland, and lived in London, until my mother died. He said that he only knew this recently, and that I must not be surprised if I saw my father in the course of six months or in less time, for he was abroad at present, and he might return in that time or in a less time, if he could leave his business.

"I had already passed the age of twenty, and I had said nothing to my employer about his daughter, after the information I had received from him about my parents, which gave me more pleasure than any news that I ever received.

"About this time an event occurred which ought to have occurred four years before. One morning a gentleman paid us some money in gold instead of giving a cheque, but he had just arrived from Germany, and had several large gold coins that he knew we would take at their full value, and the amount was about the value of ten sovereigns. This money was on one of the desks, and left there, while I stepped into the private room to have some conversation with this gentleman, and when I returned these foreign coins were gone. We had lately employed two new men to do rough work, and they were not very nice in manners. This morning there was a great deal of work to do, and there was considerable noise not far from the desk. When I came from the private room, the rascal of the house was in the room above, but soon appeared humming his old opera tune. I spoke of the absence of the coins, and he stared at me, and then at the porters. I asked the person who paid them to me if he would know them, and he said he could swear to them, for he had carried them so long, that they were as familiar to him as his watch.

"'Now, while I think of it,' said he, 'I remember one day in looking at them I scratched the letters on them which are contained in my name.' Our rascal with the wonderful eyes was in reality a miser, and one day before this occurrence I happened to be in a place rather obscure, where I saw this gentleman go into a sort of money-changing shop, and I knew that if he had stolen these coins, he would go to that very place to change them, sometime during the day, and I was not mistaken.

"He went out to attend to some business, and when he returned, I went out also, and meeting the gentleman who had paid me the coins, we procured a cab and drove to the money-changer's, who was a fat, good-natured Dutch Jew.

"The thief, like the miser he was, wanted good solid English sovereigns, and procured these before he attended to the business for the house.

"The Jew produced the foreign coins, getting a pretty good commission for his services. So he made a profit in both transactions. He said he 'vos very poor man, and he muscht live, for he had scho much bigger famalisch like oscher mens, and muscht have de moneish to schuport dem.'

"In a few minutes, we, including Mr. Moss, were in a cab, and in a few more minutes we were in the warehouse, with two policemen at each door, and with Mr. Moss inside, near the door.

"When we made our appearance the eyes of the thief and murderer (although the latter crime could not have been proved to have been committed by him,) were rather dim.

"The proprietor, who had been at the desk during my absence, was one of the number who confronted this wretched man.

"He had always drawn the full amount of his salary, at the end of every week, and as this exciting day was Monday, he was very nearly even with the house.

"When he was caught, he writhed like a snake whose head was under the foot of a man. He drew from his pocket the money which he had received from the Jew, and gave it to his master, giving me a look which made me shiver, and said to me, 'If ever I hated a person in this infernal world, I hate you, and if it were not for the disgrace of the gallows, I would kill you as soon as I would an Indian cobra.' In a whisper, so low that it could not be heard by any one but himself as I came near and bent towards him, I said, '*Johnny Wilton!*' when he fell back against the side of the building, as if he had received a mortal wound.

He soon partially raised his head, and stood leaning against the wall, looking in different ways, like a baffled hyena — portraying the worst passions of a human being; viz., despair, misery, hatred, terror, rage and revenge. Ten sovereigns were offered him by his master, which he declined to receive. He had no need for them, as he had several hundred coins of the same value. He was then warned by me that he must not be seen in any part of the United Kingdom in twenty-four hours from that time.

"When I had said this, he turned to leave the house, and when he had taken two or three steps, he turned his face towards mine, giving me a look that I shall never forget, for it is before me in the daytime, and in my dreams.

"When Mr. Moss heard my last words to his former customer, he suddenly departed, and I understood that his bank, pawnbroker's shop, or old clothes warehouse, was not opened until two days after my sentence was spoken to the unfortunate man.

"I never knew what became of my once fellow clerk, but I once thought that I saw him in Paris. If it was he, he soon disappeared in one of the narrowest streets, leading into the Avenue des Champs Elysées.

"A short time after the departure of the dishonest clerk, I received a letter from my father, desiring me to visit him at a certain hour of the day, at the hotel where he was living.

"When the day and hour arrived for this visit, with some little nervousness I went to the hotel, and sent in my card. In a few minutes I was in the presence of as fine a looking gentleman as I had ever seen.

"As I entered the room he rose from his seat, and, after looking at me for a moment, caught me in his arms, and with a voice full of emotion he said, ' Well, my dear boy, we have met at last, and we should never have parted.'

"He then passed a few compliments, which I will not repeat, as I always was a very modest person.

"I behaved as I should have done, and as I had done nothing to be ashamed of, I did not cry much.

"My father then told me how he married my mother, who was a poor, but a very beautiful girl, and they were very much attached to each other. He said that they were married in Scotland, but only a few persons knew of the marriage.

"Afterwards they lived privately in London, and about two years after I was born my mother died, and my father said that he had never been so happy as he was when they were living together.

"My father then said that he ought to have proclaimed the marriage, but like a coward, was afraid of his relations. He said that he had got over that nonsense now, and that I should be proclaimed as his son and heir.

"Six months after this I married my employer's daughter, and about the same time became a partner in the old established warehouse near the Docks."

XXVII.

THE CHEVALIER ST. GEORGE.

FROM the beginning of the reign of Charles the Second, to the accession of George the Third, a period of one hundred years, the morals of the English people were far inferior to what they have been since the termination of that period.

Cromwell governed the country with rigor, and all classes were afraid of him, at home and abroad.

But when the easy, pleasure-loving Charles the Second ascended the throne, the people were to a certain degree unrestrained, and licentiousness and petty and greater crimes were not exceptions.

When James the Second became King, instead of following the example of Charles, he, by the advice and aid of Judge Jeffreys, pursued a course which was the reverse of that of Charles.

James was of a gloomy disposition, and not popular with the people.

One day he said to Charles that he had better change his mode of life, for the people might become dissatisfied, and told him to remember his father.

Charles replied, "There is no fear, James, of the people killing or dethroning *me*, to make *you* king," and from that time James let Charles have his own way.

After James was dethroned by William and his wife, (James' eldest daughter,) William and Mary governed strictly, but well, and the people were pretty well contented — compared with their contentment during the reign of James and his dear friend Jeffreys, the latter loving the people so well that he sent them out of the world, when he had an opportunity of doing so, as a criminal judge, thinking them too good for this place, and that the sooner they were out of it the better.

When Queen Anne came to the throne, the so-called masses broke loose, for they had been under restraint long enough, and although stealing for great or small amounts was a capital crime, and more persons bid the world adieu at Tyburn than in any other period of twelve years, crimes large and small were very numerous.

The Duke of Marlborough was carrying everything before him, and it seemed as if he and Prince Eugene of Savoy could go where they pleased, and stay as long as they pleased, with or without the permission of any person or any number of persons; and some may now think that the Duke of Marlborough was the greatest of all English captains; and some of these persons may be strictly impartial regarding soldiers and civilians.

It naturally followed that there were large numbers of disbanded soldiers — some who were, and some who were not, wounded, were turned loose; after fighting in as bloody contests as had taken place since fire-arms were invented. But the morals of the people were not improved by the accession to their numbers of these discharged soldiers. Men fought gallantly in those glorious battles of Marlborough, but when they were out of the army, were different men.*

There were also some fine victories attained by the English on the sea during the short reign of Queen Anne, during twelve years. It may be truly said that her reign was short and glorious.

About fifty years after her death, a very old man died in fair circumstances, as regards his worldly

* People may erect statuary for a great general, with epitaphs, biography and sonnets, all flattering; but they should also remember the greater generals before him.

condition. In a small drawer was found a written history of a society which was called, "The Secret Organization, in the small Court near the Main Thoroughfare."

The person who wrote the history of this Society, does not state that he was a member, for the first person is never mentioned; but if he was a member, he must have been the last living one, the moment before his death, for in the history he writes of no member of the organization being younger than forty years of age, at the time when Queen Anne died.

In a small court, which is entered by a narrow street or lane, is an old house of three stories, built of brick and stone, with small windows and large doors; this house and surroundings having an ancient appearance.

All of the houses in the court were said to have been built in the reign of Edward the Fourth, and afterwards a wide street was made near this court, which became the main thoroughfare.

The house had been vacant for more than six months, when it was taken by the main organizer of the Society.

At the beginning of the reign of Queen Anne, this

Society was formed for the purpose of placing the son of James the Second, the King *de jure*, (known as the Chevalier St. George,) on the throne of England.

The house in the small court was the most suitable place for the meetings, as it would escape the observation of persons living in the main streets, or in the narrow streets and alleys near the court.

On the ground-floor there was a door leading to an alley in the rear of the house; this alley led to a narrow street which had a number of streets leading to it, one of these leading to the main thoroughfare. This door had every appearance of being a permanently closed door or large window from the outside, and from the inside of the house it would never be noticed, for it had the uniform appearance of the other parts of the wall, which were not in a very good condition.

The chief organizer of the party, in looking at the room when hiring the house, and remarking on the bad condition of the wall, happened to rap with his walking-stick on the place where the supposed closed door or window was situated. He did not mention his discovery at the time; but, as soon as he was alone, tried the door and opened it without much difficulty, and as soon as the Society was formed, every member was made acquainted with the new way of exit, which was only to be made in a case of emergency.

The number of members at first was fifteen, eventually increased to twenty-seven. No less number than the first which composed the organization, was known until the year when the Chevalier St. George embarked at Montrose, for France, after having been entirely unsuccessful in his expedition, and to the great grief, mortification and disappointment of the Secret Society, and when they met, such weeping, tearing of hair, recriminations and execrations, were never heard before or since within the walls of the house in the small court. Two of the members had lost their lives at the battle of Dunblane, and three more were wounded, but not seriously. Some of the members execrated the Earl of Mar, and some the Pretender, (as he was called by the King *de facto* and his adherents,) and some execrated both of them.

When the Chevalier arrived in Scotland, the fighting was all over, and about the first thing that he did after this was to get away again as soon as possible, and the little French ship at Montrose was in the right place at exactly the right time, for this.

All of this trouble occurred in the early part of the reign of George the First; but the Chevalier, in the reign of Queene Anne, had attempted to land in Scotland, but having seen some English ships that he supposed were after him, concluded to go back to France.

It was not for any personal love for the Chevalier St. George, that the secret society espoused his cause; it was the love they had always borne for his mother, Mary of Modena, and for their love of the Catholic faith. They all thought that this religion ought to be the religion of Europe, and that the Church should be supreme and have unlimited power.

When the Society was organized, every member was to be unmarried, and no one was to be dependent on any of them for support; but at any time, if any members wished to marry, they must notify every other member, and then withdraw from the Society and never enter the house where the meetings were held.

The rules regarding traitors were such that there was no danger of any one of the organization, (unless he should become a lunatic,) giving any information to the Government regarding the movements of the

Society, or of the party who were working for the Chevalier. There were none of the members, who ever betrayed their comrades; but there were a number of persons of the other party, who did not belong to the Society, who had better been quiet, and not have meddled with the adherents of the son of James the Second, the king *de jure*.

The members of the organization were supposed to have some regular occupation, and they must be so situated that they must appear to be engaged when any one entered their rooms, which were in various parts of the city; thus some appeared to be engaged in one occupation, and some in another; but in reality, they did little or nothing. After doing all that they possibly could do for the great cause — and for this cause no crime was too great for them to risk their honor, if they had any, or their lives — and when every soul of them knew that there were large numbers of persons who were executed at Tyburn, whose places should have been filled by the members and some others of their party, these members sometimes felt a little grim and insecure.

Every night before eight o'clock, each had to show himself if he was in the city and not ill; but there was no letter writing, and no messages were sent. One old Catholic acted as the servant, did his work well, and held his tongue; but for any one to say a word against the Old faith, or to doubt the infallibility of the Pope, was the greatest of all crimes to him. Most of the members were poor, but plenty of money was supplied to the organization, and this came from all parts of Catholic Europe. To avoid suspicion, there were musical instruments in the rooms, and there were some good performers and vocalists, who, at times were quite enlivening to that dismal neighborhood. Cards, chess, and draughts were sometimes played.

If any of the members were arrested, no influence of the Catholic party, either at home or abroad, nor any amount of money, was spared to procure his liberty.

During the reign of Queen Anne, and until the Chevalier embarked at Montrose for France, every one of the organization had his duties to perform — some in London, and in various parts of England and Scotland — visiting London frequently; and others were abroad, mostly in France. They all worked and worked hard; and if the leaders of the Catholic party had done *their* duty, there might have been better results.

The most zealous of the society had knelt before the Pope, receiving his blessing, and had assisted the exiled king's wife, when she retreated, (on the advent of William and Mary,) from England, receiving also her blessing.

When he first saw her, she was standing on the banks of the river, being greatly agitated and in tears. The little Chevalier was much frightened and clung to his mother, crying as only a frightened child could cry, and stout, rough-appearing men cried like children.

When we consider the fact of a King being deposed and driven from his country, and his lovely Queen, (with his child,) standing on the banks of the Thames, waiting for a boat, with a number of persons — who were mostly of a rough appearance — we cannot wonder at the friends of the ruined King and Queen espousing their cause.

In Queen Anne's reign, at various times, a number of persons came to the house in the small court for refuge, and when the house was searched, made their exit through the secret door, which was opened and closed in a few moments; all being done almost as soon as the knocking on the public door in the court had ceased.

The active member had received as a present from persons abroad, some diamonds, which were valued at several thousand guineas, and as he wanted money, he sold them to a Jew, to whom he said that the diamonds were a present from some friends; but the Israelite, whose eyes glittered — like the eyes of a snake — when he saw the precious gems, evidently thought they had been stolen; and during the negotiations for their transfer, Mr. Ishmael intimated to the owner of the diamonds that he was greatly indebted to him for offering to buy them at any price, as it was a dangerous proceeding. The owner told him that if he ever should be so unfortunate as to be compelled to pay a visit to Tyburn, Mr. Moses Ishmael would be there to receive him — unless he should conclude to wander like his namesake of old, through the desert. The Jew said he "was only shoking, and that the proprietor of the shewels could never take a shoke."

The diamonds were finally sold to the Jew, and the money obtained for them enabled their former owner to live in ease and comfort to the end of his life.

After the unsuccessful attempt of the Chevalier de St. George to ascend the English throne, the partisans abandoned nearly all of their hopes of the Stuart restoration; and one night, ten of the members of the secret organization were alarmed by a loud knocking at the door in the court, and by looking through the blinds, a number of soldiers were seen. The secret door was opened and closed, as the entire party, (including the old servant,) made their exit, and from that time there no longer existed the secret organization in the small court near the main thoroughfare.

XXVIII.

HYDE PARK IN SEVERAL REIGNS.

DURING the reign of Charles I., Hyde Park was opened to the public as a pleasure ground, and during his reign there were horse and foot races in the place, which were seen and enjoyed by the King and the Royal Party.

There was a gentleman named Henry Marten, an M. P., who was disliked by the King. When the Monarch saw him, he said quite loud, "Let that ugly man leave the Park, or I will not stay to see the sport." Mr. Marten was said to have signed his name next to Cromwell's when the King was condemned.

Our author states that Cromwell threw ink in Marten's face, as a joke, and that Marten returned the compliment by smearing Cromwell's face in rough return, but the story has to be taken only for just what it is worth.

In the first year of the Civil War, a fort was erected where Hamilton Place, Piccadilly, now stands, which was mostly built by the money and energy of ladies of title, who were intensely loyal to King Charles. This fort was demolished in 1647 by order of the House of Commons, as there was no further use for it.

At the north-eastern corner of Hyde Park, a guard-house was erected, and a close watch was kept over all who went along the road to Oxford, where the Court then resided.

One day, a poor man named Thomas Fuller, an obscure lecturer at the Savoy, was arrested, who showed a pass from the Parliament to the vigilant sentries, but the Captain of the Guard said he would see that he did carry nothing but what he had a warrant for. Several petitions to the King and other papers were found in the pockets of the lecturer, and he was taken back to Parliament by a troop of soldiers.

The Park during these troubled times continued a place of public resort, but in 1645, orders were given that it should be kept shut, and that no person be allowed to go into it, on Sundays, Fast and Thanksgiving days.

On the 31st of May, 1650, there was a great military display in the Park. His Highness, the Lord Lieutenant of Ireland, Oliver Cromwell by name, returned to London, after the wars in that country. As he passed through the Park, the great guns fired salutes, whilst one regiment, which was drawn up, fired a volley. A flatterer was said to have remarked to Oliver, that he seemed to have the voice of the people, as well as the voice of God. "As to God," replied Cromwell, "We will not talk about him here, but for the people, they would be just as noisy if they were going to see me hanged."

In 1658 Cromwell died, and was buried in Westminster Abbey, where his remains rested until 1660, when they were dug up, hanged on a gibbet, quartered and burnt, by orders of Charles the Second.

On the accession of Charles, Hyde Park soon became what it had been before the Civil War, the rendezvous of fashion, and very soon after the members of the Royal family were safely lodged in the palaces of St. James and Whitehall, when they commenced their round of amusements, Hyde Park forming part of the programme.

At that time the new riding garb, the Amazone, as it was called, came into fashion, and the present long-skirted habit is said to have originated from the Amazone. Until then the ladies had worn the usual walking-dress on horseback.

There was at this time a place called The Ring, where the people of fashion used to drive, and it was sometimes called The Tour.

During the reign of Charles II., he sometimes reviewed the troops in Hyde Park. They were nearly all young men of a handsome appearance, and the uniform was gallant and picturesque in the extreme. They wore round cavalier hats, with a profusion of white feathers, scarlet coats covered with gold lace; wide sleeves slashed in front; large white linen collars turned over the neck; scarlet sashes round their waists; jack-boots coming up very high, and large ruffles round the waist. Their horses were all black. and the long tails on field-days were tied up with ribbons, which also ornamented their heads and manes. These ribbons in the first troop were blue, in the second green, and in the third yellow. In this gaudy costume they must have presented a splendid sight, as they rode past the King.

Coaches with glass window were invented at this time, but the ladies did not like being shut up in them, for they could not show themselves.

The Park was very dull in 1665, which was the year of the Great Plague, and the greater part of the fashionable world left the metropolis, and even the kingdom, but two or three years after, everything was as lively as ever.

There were games of all kinds in the Park in the reigns of Charles the First and his sons, and shows and reviews; in fact almost every variety of amusement, and people were frequently known, in pleasant weather, to spend the entire day in the place, as they do now in the Parks in France.

In the reigns of James the Second, and William and Mary, the Park had lost something of its gayety, but still the people went there to drive, ride and walk, and there were military reviews. Sometime in the year 1700, two captains of the guards fought a duel with swords and one of them was killed, and in the following year a colonel was killed by a captain, and about ten years after, a duel was fought by a duke and another peer in the same place, and both died shortly after the combat.

In 1715, there were several Roman Catholic riots in London, when George I. was insulted, and also his followers. The friends of the Stuarts were rejoicing in the hope of the restoration of that banished dynasty, and were praising and celebrating the birthday of James the Second's son. The Protestant party retaliated by burning the Pretender in effigy, and the Stuart faction did the same by King William. During the reign of Queen Anne, St. James's Park was the place for military executions, but a few took place in Hyde Park, and some were flogged there for insubordination.

In 1723, there was a grand review on the King's birthday, and a large amount of mutton, beef and beer were given to the soldiers. George I., and all of the other Kings of that name knew well how to conciliate the people, and that the best way to gain the good will of the masses was to give them plenty of good provisions.

The Serpentine was formed during the reign of George II., about the year 1735, but a number of improvements have been made on it since. The old Ring or drive, was deserted shortly after the grand road for equestrians and that for carriages were opened, about 1738. The latter was called Rotten Row, several years afterwards.

About, 1750 several people were robbed in their carriages, on horseback and on foot. Many of the highwaymen were arrested and executed at Tyburn, in view of the scene of their misdeeds.

HYDE PARK IN SEVERAL REIGNS. 205

When George III. came to the throne, duelling was still the rage, and John Wilkes, who appeared to be always in trouble about something, fought a duel with a Mr. Martin, M. P. for Camelford. The duel was fought with pistols and Wilkes was wounded.

In the early part of the reign of George III., during a very severe frost, the snow covered the entire country, and sleds were hastily constructed like those in Norway and other cold countries.

Duels continued during the greater part of the reign of George III. One of the latest was fought in 1803, between two officers in the English army, one of whom was killed.

The American trouble began in earnest in 1775, and Hyde Park was used in a great measure for drilling men for soldiers, who "were going to give the Colonists a lesson that they would not forget in a hurry." They were going to let the Dutch Hessians commence the work, and set the Americans running; the British Invincibles would come in and catch them, and bring them all to England, when the war would be over. Somehow or other, this game was not won, and they said if General so-and-so had done differently, there would have been better results. There was always something the matter with their generals on land, and something generally wrong with their admirals on the water, both in 1775 and 1814.

The Parks were used extensively for camps during the Lord George Gordon riots in 1780; but these lasted only about four days. In that time, a large amount of property was destroyed and several lives lost. Lord George Gordon feared that the Roman Catholics would obtain the ascendency, but as they did not constitute one-fifth of the population in England and Scotland, his fears would seem to have been groundless.

Sunday was the fashionable day for Hyde Park, but, as may be supposed, there was a general mixture of people, and the people in England were as well represented then in the Park as they are now at the Races.

In the year 1798, a regiment was formed which was called "The ragged regiment of cavalry." They were said to have been the most motley crowd that ever took the field. Men of all sizes, from the smallest that could be found in the kingdom to the largest, with the smallest and largest horses that could be obtained in the country. The smallest men were placed on immense horses, and the largest men *vice versâ*. There was no attempt to uniform them. Every one dressed to please himself, but the organization only lasted for a short time.

The fashions of the ladies' dresses at this time were probably more absurd than they have been in any age, and the other sex were not very far behind in absurdity in dress. It would be almost impossible to give anything like an accurate description of the fashionable dresses of ladies and gentlemen of that period.

About 1816, the Park was not in the condition that it is at the present time, and the roads and walks were few in comparison with those of the present.

Chairs were admitted into the Park in the early part of the reign of George IV. There has probably not been much change in Hyde Park for the last fifty years, with the exception of better roads, and a larger collection of trees, shrubs and flowers.

XXIX.

VARIETIES OF POPULAR AMUSEMENTS.

THE ENGLISH people, as a class, are the most conventional in the world, and their customs and amusements are continued from one generation to another, with a persistency unparalleled by any other people.

In all amusements, including horse-racing, fox-hunting, cricket playing, rowing, and other recreations, the same interest is undoubtedly manifested at the present time, as was manifested a hundred years ago, and in some amusements there is more pleasure derived from them now than there has ever been since they were first invented.

If a gentleman wishes to sell his fox-hounds, there is always a buyer for them who will pay a good price, and I have been informed by an English gentleman, that he has never known a fox-hunting station to become extinct, but on the contrary, has known many new ones formed. Whatever misfortune may happen to the country, this sport is sure to be maintained.

If a farmer objects to have the hunters riding through his wheat fields, he becomes unpopular — not only with the gentry and their families, but by all others in the country, or wherever he is known. His name is sure to appear in the newspapers, and he is execrated by all sportsmen, and the sooner he makes an humble apology by removing the obstacle, the better for him; otherwise he might as well leave the country and never return, for he will have no peace at home.

Ladies sometimes ride after the hounds, and have been the first, or among the first, nearest the fox when he is killed. The English ladies are undoubtedly the finest equestrians in the world.

At all of the races the number of the people increases every year, with more horses, and more profits and losses, and more everlasting ruin to a large number of people.

I once went to the Derby, and it was a sight for one who had never before seen a great English horse-race. The newspapers reported the many thousands of persons who were on the grounds that day. Some classes are never seen at any other place, except by their companions, or by the police. How they get there, or what they do when they get there, or how they manage to get away, they may know, but others do not know. Some are masses of rags, without shoes, and some are without hats. They hang around the restaurants, to see if they cannot pick up some pieces of bread and meat which may be thrown to them, or to find some which has fallen to the ground.

I saw a young man who was under a table, and he found the bone of a mutton cutlet, which he seized, eating the small amount of meat remaining on the bone, as eagerly as a hungry dog. A few feet from this young man, were persons in rich equipages, who apparently had every thing that money or credit could procure.

The custom of gambling in public places has been abolished in spite of conventionalism, and is not likely to be re-established. But more is lost at one of the races in a day than ever was lost in one gambling house for a month. There is not much difference between the two, only one is the betting place and the other is the gambling place. As far as the results are concerned, there would seem to be a distinction without a difference.

When we hear of gambling-houses being suppressed,

VARIETIES OF POPULAR AMUSEMENTS. 211

and other evils following in their train, and then see one of these races patronized by the highest in the land, a disinterested person cannot help thinking that these horse-races should follow, either among the last or in the rear.

The boat-races on the Thames in April are more popular than ever, and probably will be more popular in the future than they have been in the past. The boats are rowed from Putney to Mortlake, which is about four miles, and for that distance on the day of the race the banks of the river are lined with people. Every house is filled, or every house would be filled if the occupants would allow the spectators to fill them, and steamboats and every style of craft are full of people. The ladies wear the colors of the boat crews,— a light blue for Cambridge and a darker blue for Oxford. When the news of the result arrives, the friends of both parties are in the same spirits as people usually are in all contests.

Cricket playing is a very popular amusement in England, the game being played by pretty large men, middle-sized men, youths, boys and small boys. Sometimes they bat each other instead of batting the ball, but only by accident, of course.

The American game of pools is played but very little in England, and it is not popular when it is played.

At the opera, in England as in other countries, the people are seen in their best colors, or I should say in their best style, and the sight is very imposing, or to use another word, very grand. Some of the young gentlemen with their lorgnettes seem to watch the motions of others when the applause and *encore* are given, rather more than they do their own emotions.

Mr. Adolphus Fitz Noodle watches very carefully where the applause comes from, before he consents to join, for if it comes from the regions far above, Adolphus is mute, and is engaged with the lorgnette.

For a long period of time, it was the custom to walk in the Park on Sunday afternoons, and on that day there were more pedestrians in the place than on any other day of the week. But the people became more promiscuous every year, and the best classes remain at home on Sunday afternoons, or visit other places more select.

About three years ago, some of the persons who lived in Park Lane and Belgravia, met in a quiet part of the Park on Sunday afternoons, and as they found it very pleasant to see their friends in a charming place, they concluded to continue these meetings. As soon as this fact was known, the numbers who visited the place in a few weeks, were larger than they had ever been, and among the thousands, were a large number of persons of a very attractive appearance.

This was one of the few old customs, for a short time abolished, but was sensibly and happily restored.

In the last month of autumn, the Park is nearly deserted, the flowers have been removed, the leaves are falling from the trees, and many persons who have visited this Elysian field, will be seen there no more, but, like the leaves that fall, their places will be filled by others in the coming spring.

THE END.

T. B. PETERSON AND BROTHERS' NEW BOOKS.

Booksellers, News Agents, and all others in want of good and fast-selling books will please send in their orders at once.

ÉMILE ZOLA'S NEW AND GREAT WORKS.

L'Assommoir. By *Emile Zola*. The Greatest Novel ever printed. Price 75 cents in paper cover, or $1.00 in morocco cloth, black and gold.

The Markets of Paris; or, *Le Ventre de Paris*. By *Emile Zola*. Price 75 cents in paper cover, or $1.25 in morocco cloth, black and gold.

The Conquest of Plassans; or, *La Conquete de Plassans*. By *Emile Zola*. Price 75 cents in paper cover, or $1.25 in cloth, black and gold.

The Rougon-Macquart Family; or, *La Fortune Des Rougon*. By *Emile Zola*. Price 75 cents in paper cover, or $1.25 in cloth, black and gold.

The Abbé's Temptation; or, *La Faute De L'Abbe Mouret*. By *Emile Zola*. Price 75 cents in paper cover, or $1.25 in cloth, black and gold.

Hélène, a Love Episode; or, *Une Page D'Amour*. By *Emile Zola*. Price 75 cents in paper cover, or $1.25 in morocco cloth, black and gold.

HENRY GREVILLE'S GREAT NOVELS.

Dosia. A *Russian Story*. By *Henry Gréville*, author of "Markof."
Philomène's Marriages. With Author's Preface. By *Henry Gréville*.
Pretty Little Countess Zina. By *Henry Gréville*, author of "Dosia."
Marrying Off a Daughter. A *Love Story*. By *Henry Gréville*.

Above are in paper cover, price 75 cents each, or in cloth, at $1.25 each.

Savéli's Expiation. A Powerful Novel. By Henry Gréville.
Dournof. A Russian Story. By Henry Gréville, author of "Dosia."
Bonne-Marie. A Tale of Normandy and Paris. By Henry Gréville.
A Friend; or, "L'Ami." By Henry Gréville, author of "Dosia."
Sonia. A Love Story. By Henry Gréville, author of "Dosia."
Gabrielle; or, The House of Maurèze. By Henry Gréville.

Above are in paper cover, price 50 cents each, or in cloth, at $1.00 each.

Markof, the Russian Violinist. A Russian Story. By Henry Gréville. One large volume, 12mo., cloth, price $1.50, or paper cover, 75 cents.

MRS. BURNETT'S LOVE STORIES.

Kathleen. A Love Story. By Mrs. Frances Hodgson Burnett.
A Quiet Life. By Mrs. Frances Hodgson Burnett, author of "Theo."
Miss Crespigny. A Charming Love Story. By author of "Kathleen."
Theo. A Love Story. By author of "Kathleen," "Miss Crespigny," etc.
Pretty Polly Pemberton. By author of "Kathleen," "Theo," etc.

Above are in paper cover, price 50 cents each, or in cloth, at $1.00 each.

Jarl's Daughter and Other Tales. By Mrs. Burnett. Price 25 cents.
Lindsay's Luck. By Mrs. Frances Hodgson Burnett. Price 25 cents.

☞ Above Books will be sent, postage paid, on receipt of Retail Price, by T. B. Peterson & Brothers, Philadelphia, Pa.   (A)

T. B. PETERSON AND BROTHERS' NEW BOOKS.

BY AUTHOR OF "A HEART TWICE WON."

A Heart Twice Won; or, Second Love. *A Love Story.* By Mrs. Elizabeth Van Loon. Morocco cloth, black and gold. Price $1.50.
Under the Willows; or, The Three Countesses. *By Mrs. Elizabeth Van Loon*, author of "A Heart Twice Won." Cloth, and gold. Price $1.50.
The Shadow of Hampton Mead. *A Charming Story.* By Mrs. Elizabeth Van Loon, author of "A Heart Twice Won." Cloth. Price $1.50.

NEW AND GOOD BOOKS BY BEST AUTHORS.

The Earl of Mayfield. *Fourth Edition Now Ready.* Complete in one large duodecimo volume, morocco cloth, black and gold, price $1.50.
The Last Athenian. By Victor Rydberg. Translated from the Swedish. Large 12mo. volume, near 600 pages, cloth, black and gold, price $1.75.
The Count de Camors. *The Man of the Second Empire.* By Octave Feuillet. Price 75 cents in paper cover, or $1.25 in morocco cloth.
The Amours of Phillippe; or, Phillippe's Love Affairs. *By Octave Feuillet.* Price 50 cents in paper, or $1.00 in cloth, black and gold.
Major Jones's Courtship. *Author's New, Rewritten, and Enlarged Edition.* By Major Joseph Jones. 21 Illustrations. Price 75 cents.
Rancy Cottem's Courtship. By author of "Major Jones's Courtship." *Author's Edition.* 8 Illustrations. Price 50 cents.

NEW BOOKS BY THE VERY BEST AUTHORS.

The following books are all printed on tinted paper, and are each issued in uniform style, in square 12mo. form. Price Fifty Cents each in Paper Cover, or $1.00 each in Morocco Cloth, Black and Gold.

Sybil Brotherton. A Novel. By Mrs. Emma D. E. N. Southworth.
The Red Hill Tragedy. By Mrs. Emma D. E. N. Southworth.
Fanchon, the Cricket; or, La Petite Fadette. By George Sand. *This is the work from which the play of "Fanchon, the Cricket," is dramatized.*
Carmen. By Prosper Merimee. *The original work, from which the popular Opera of "Carmen," as presented on the stage, was dramatized.*
Miss Margery's Roses. A Charming Love Story. By Robert C. Meyers.
The Days of Madame Pompadour. By Gabrielle De St. Andre.
Father Tom and the Pope; or, A Night at the Vatican. Illustrated.
Madeleine. A Charming Love Story. Jules Sandeau's Prize Novel.
Madame Pompadour's Garter. A Romance of the Reign of Louis XV.
A Woman's Mistake; or, Jacques de Trévannes. A Charming Love Story.
The Story of Elizabeth. By Miss Thackeray, daughter of W. M. Thackeray.
The Matchmaker. By Beatrice Reynolds. A Charming Love Story.
Two Ways to Matrimony; or, Is it Love? or, False Pride.
That Girl of Mine. By the author of "That Lover of Mine."
Bessie's Six Lovers. A Charming Love Story. By Henry Peterson.
That Lover of Mine. By the author of "That Girl of Mine."

Above are in paper cover, price 50 cents each, or in cloth, at $1.00 each.

☞ Above Books will be sent, postage paid, on Receipt of Retail Price, by T. B. Peterson & Brothers, Philadelphia, Pa.

T. B. PETERSON AND BROTHERS' PUBLICATIONS.

☞ Orders solicited from Booksellers, Librarians, News Agents, and all others in want of good and fast-selling books. ☜

MRS. EMMA D. E. N. SOUTHWORTH'S WORKS.

Complete in forty-three large duodecimo volumes, bound in morocco cloth, gilt back, price $1.75 each; or $75.25 a set, each set is put up in a neat box.

The Phantom Wedding; or, The Fall of the House of Flint,	$1 75		
Self-Raised; From the Depths..	$1 75	The Fatal Marriage,	1 75
Ishmael; or, In the Depths,	1 75	The Deserted Wife,	1 75
The Mother-in-Law,	1 75	The Fortune Seeker,	1 75
The Fatal Secret,	1 75	The Bridal Eve,	1 75
How He Won Her,	1 75	The Lost Heiress,	1 75
Fair Play,	1 75	The Two Sisters,	1 75
The Spectre Lover,	1 75	Lady of the Isle,	1 75
Victor's Triumph,	1 75	Prince of Darkness,	1 75
A Beautiful Fiend,	1 75	The Three Beauties,	1 75
The Artist's Love,	1 75	Vivia; or the Secret of Power,	1 75
A Noble Lord,	1 75	Love's Labor Won,	1 75
Lost Heir of Linlithgow,	1 75	The Gipsy's Prophecy,	1 75
Tried for her Life,	1 75	Retribution,	1 75
Cruel as the Grave,	1 75	The Christmas Guest,	1 75
The Maiden Widow,	1 75	Haunted Homestead,	1 75
The Family Doom,	1 75	Wife's Victory,	1 75
The Bride's Fate,	1 75	Allworth Abbey,	1 75
The Changed Brides,	1 75	India; Pearl of Pearl River,	1 75
Fallen Pride,	1 75	Curse of Clifton,	1 75
The Widow's Son,	1 75	Discarded Daughter,	1 75
The Bride of Llewellyn,	1 75	The Mystery of Dark Hollow,	1 75
The Missing Bride; or, Miriam, the Avenger,			1 75

Above are each in cloth, or each one is in paper cover, at $1.50 each.

MRS. CAROLINE LEE HENTZ'S WORKS.

Green and Gold Edition. Complete in twelve volumes, in green morocco cloth, price $1.75 each; or $21.00 a set, each set is put up in a neat box.

Ernest Linwood,	$1 75	Love after Marriage,	$1 75
The Planter's Northern Bride,	1 75	Eoline; or Magnolia Vale,	1 75
Courtship and Marriage,	1 75	The Lost Daughter,	1 75
Rena; or, the Snow Bird,	1 75	The Banished Son,	1 75
Marcus Warland,	1 75	Helen and Arthur,	1 75
Linda; or, the Young Pilot of the Belle Creole,			1 75
Robert Graham; the Sequel to "Linda; or Pilot of Belle Creole,"			1 75

Above are each in cloth, or each one is in paper cover, at $1.50 each.

☞ Above Books will be sent, postage paid, on receipt of Retail Price by T. B. Peterson & Brothers, Philadelphia, Pa. (1)

MRS. ANN S. STEPHENS' WORKS.

Complete in twenty-three large duodecimo volumes, bound in morocco cloth, gilt back, price $1.75 each; or $40.25 a set, each set is put up in a neat box.

Norston's Rest,	$1 75	The Soldiers' Orphans,	$1 75
Bertha's Engagement,	1 75	A Noble Woman,	1 75
Bellehood and Bondage,	1 75	Silent Struggles,	1 75
The Old Countess,	1 75	The Rejected Wife,	1 75
Lord Hope's Choice,	1 75	The Wife's Secret,	1 75
The Reigning Belle,	1 75	Mary Derwent,	1 75
Palaces and Prisons,	1 75	Fashion and Famine,	1 75
Married in Haste,	1 75	The Curse of Gold,	1 75
Wives and Widows,	1 75	Mabel's Mistake,	1 75
Ruby Gray's Strategy,	1 75	The Old Homestead,	1 75
Doubly False,	1 75	The Heiress,... 1 75	The Gold Brick,... 1 75

Above are each in cloth, or each one is in paper cover, at $1.50 each.

MRS. C. A. WARFIELD'S WORKS.

Complete in nine large duodecimo volumes, bound in morocco cloth, gilt back, price $1.75 each; or $15.75 a set, each set is put up in a neat box.

The Cardinal's Daughter,	$1 75	Miriam's Memoirs,	$1 75
Ferne Fleming,	1 75	Monfort Hall,	1 75
The Household of Bouverie,	1 75	Sea and Shore,	1 75
A Double Wedding,	1 75	Hester Howard's Temptation,	1 75
Lady Ernestine; or, The Absent Lord of Rocheforte,			1 75

BEST COOK BOOKS PUBLISHED.

Every housekeeper should possess at least one of the following Cook Books, as they would save the price of it in a week's cooking.

The Queen of the Kitchen. Containing 1007 Old Maryland Family Receipts for Cooking,	Cloth,	$1 75
Miss Leslie's New Cookery Book,	Cloth,	1 75
Mrs. Hale's New Cook Book,	Cloth,	1 75
Petersons' New Cook Book,	Cloth,	1 75
Widdifield's New Cook Book,	Cloth,	1 75
Mrs. Goodfellow's Cookery as it Should Be,	Cloth,	1 75
The National Cook Book. By a Practical Housewife,	Cloth,	1 75
The Young Wife's Cook Book,	Cloth,	1 75
Miss Leslie's New Receipts for Cooking,	Cloth,	1 75
Mrs. Hale's Receipts for the Million,	Cloth,	1 75
The Family Save-All. By author of "National Cook Book,"	Cloth,	1 75
Francatelli's Modern Cook. With the most approved methods of French, English, German, and Italian Cookery. With Sixty-two Illustrations. One volume of 600 pages, bound in morocco cloth,		5 00

☞ Above Books will be sent, postage paid, on receipt of **Retail Price,** by T. B. Peterson & Brothers, Philadelphia, Pa.

MISS ELIZA A. DUPUY'S WORKS.

Complete in fourteen large duodecimo volumes, bound in morocco cloth, gilt back, price $1.75 each; or $24.50 a set, each set is put up in a neat box.

A New Way to Win a Fortune	$1 75	Why Did He Marry Her?	$1 75
The Discarded Wife,	1 75	Who Shall be Victor?	1 75
The Clandestine Marriage,	1 75	The Mysterious Guest,	1 75
The Hidden Sin,	1 75	Was He Guilty?	1 75
The Dethroned Heiress,	1 75	The Cancelled Will,	1 75
The Gipsy's Warning,	1 75	The Planter's Daughter,	1 75
All For Love,	1 75	Michael Rudolph,	1 75

Above are each in cloth, or each one is in paper cover, at $1.50 each.

DOESTICKS' WORKS.

Complete in four large duodecimo volumes, bound in cloth, gilt back, price $1.75 each; or $7.00 a set, each set is put up in a neat box.

Doesticks' Letters,	$1 75	The Elephant Club,	$1 75
Plu-Ri-Bus-Tah,	1 75	Witches of New York,	1 75

Above are each in cloth, or each one is in paper cover, at $1.50 each.

JAMES A. MAITLAND'S WORKS.

Complete in seven large duodecimo volumes, bound in cloth, gilt back, price $1.75 each; or $12.25 a set, each set is put up in a neat box.

The Watchman,	$1 75	Diary of an Old Doctor,	$1 75
The Wanderer,	1 75	Sartaroe,	1 75
The Lawyer's Story,	1 75	The Three Cousins,	1 75
The Old Patroon; or the Great Van Broek Property,			1 75

Above are each in cloth, or each one is in paper cover, at $1.50 each.

T. ADOLPHUS TROLLOPE'S WORKS.

Complete in seven large duodecimo volumes, bound in cloth, gilt back, price $1.75 each; or $12.25 a set, each set is put up in a neat box.

The Sealed Packet,	$1 75	Dream Numbers,	$1 75
Garstang Grange,	1 75	Beppo, the Conscript,	1 75
Leonora Casaloni,	1 75	Gemma, 1 75	Marietta, 1 75

Above are each in cloth, or each one is in paper cover, at $1.50 each.

FREDRIKA BREMER'S WORKS.

Complete in six large duodecimo volumes, bound in cloth, gilt back, price $1.75 each; or $10.50 a set, each set is put up in a neat box.

Father and Daughter,	$1 75	The Neighbors,	$1 75
The Four Sisters,	1 75	The Home,	1 75

Above are each in cloth, or each one is in paper cover, at $1.50 each.

Life in the Old World. In two volumes, cloth, price, ... 3 50

☞ Above Books will be sent postage paid, on receipt of Retail Price, by T. B. Peterson & Brothers, Philadelphia, Pa.

T. B. PETERSON & BROTHERS' PUBLICATIONS.

WILKIE COLLINS' BEST WORKS.

Basil; or, The Crossed Path..$1 50 | The Dead Secret. 12mo........$1 50
Above are each in one large duodecimo volume, bound in cloth.
The Dead Secret, 8vo............... 75 | The Queen's Revenge,............... 75
Basil; or, the Crossed Path,...... 75 | Miss or Mrs?........................... 50
Hide and Seek,........................ 75 | Mad Monkton,.......................... 50
After Dark,............................ 75 | Sights a-Foot,......................... 50
The Stolen Mask,........ 25 | The Yellow Mask,... 25 | Sister Rose,... 25
The above books are each issued in paper cover, in octavo form.

FRANK FORRESTER'S SPORTING BOOK.

Frank Forrester's Sporting Scenes and Characters. By Henry William Herbert. With Illustrations by Darley. Two vols., cloth,...$4 00

EMERSON BENNETT'S WORKS.

Complete in seven large duodecimo volumes, bound in cloth, gilt back, price $1.75 each; or $12.25 a set, each set is put up in a neat box.

The Border Rover,...............$1 75 | Bride of the Wilderness,........$1 75
Clara Moreland,................. 1 75 | Ellen Norbury,.................... 1 75
The Orphan's Trials,............. 1 75 | Kate Clarendon,................... 1 75
Viola; or Adventures in the Far South-West,............................... 1 75
Above are each in cloth, or each one is in paper cover, at $1.50 each.

The Heiress of Bellefonte,...... 75 | The Pioneer's Daughter,........ 75

GREEN'S WORKS ON GAMBLING.

Complete in four large duodecimo volumes, bound in cloth, gilt back, price $1.75 each; or $7.00 a set, each set is put up in a neat box.

Gambling Exposed,..............$1 75 | Reformed Gambler,...............$1 75
The Gambler's Life,............. 1 75 | Secret Band of Brothers,........ 1 75
Above are each in cloth, or each one is in paper cover, at $1.50 each.

DOW'S PATENT SERMONS.

Complete in four large duodecimo volumes, bound in cloth, gilt back, price $1.50 each; or $6.00 a set, each set is put up in a neat box.

Dow's Patent Sermons, 1st Series, cloth,..................$1 50
Dow's Patent Sermons, 2d Series, cloth,.................. 1 50
Dow's Patent Sermons, 3d Series, cloth, ...$1 50
Dow's Patent Sermons, 4th Series, cloth,...................... 1 50
Above are each in cloth, or each one is in paper cover, at $1.00 each.

MISS BRADDON'S WORKS.

Aurora Floyd,...................... 75 | The Lawyer's Secret,............. 25
Aurora Floyd, cloth............... 1 00 | For Better, For Worse,.......... 75

☞ Above books will be sent, postage paid, on receipt of **Retail Price**, by T. B. Peterson & Brothers, Philadelphia, Pa.

CHARLES LEVER'S BEST WORKS.

Charles O'Malley,	75	Arthur O'Leary,	75
Harry Lorrequer,	75	Con Cregan,	75
Jack Hinton,	75	Davenport Dunn,	75
Tom Burke of Ours,	75	Horace Templeton,	75
Knight of Gwynne,	75	Kate O'Donoghue,	75

Above are in paper cover, or a fine edition is in cloth at $2.00 each.

A Rent in a Cloud, ... 50 | St. Patrick's Eve, ... 50

Ten Thousand a Year, in one volume, paper cover, $1.50; or in cloth, 2 00
The Diary of a Medical Student, by author "Ten Thousand a Year," 75

MRS. HENRY WOOD'S BEST BOOKS.

The Master of Greylands,	$1 50	The Shadow of Ashlydyat,	$1 50
Within the Maze,	1 50	Squire Trevlyn's Heir,	1 50
Dene Hollow,	1 50	Oswald Cray,	1 50
Bessy Rane,	1 50	Mildred Arkell,	1 50
George Canterbury's Will,	1 50	The Red Court Farm,	1 50
Verner's Pride,	1 50	Elster's Folly,	1 50
The Channings,	1 50	Saint Martin's Eve,	1 50
Roland Yorke. A Sequel to "The Channings,"			1 50
Lord Oakburn's Daughters; or, The Earl's Heirs,			1 50
The Castle's Heir; or, Lady Adelaide's Oath,			1 50

The above are each in paper cover, or in cloth, price $1.75 each.

Edina; or, Missing Since Midnight, cloth, $1, paper cover,			75
The Mystery,	75	A Life's Secret,	50
Parkwater. Told in Twilight,	75	The Haunted Tower,	50
The Lost Bank Note,	50	The Runaway Match,	25
The Lost Will,	50	Martyn Ware's Temptation,	25
Orville College,	50	The Dean of Denham,	25
Five Thousand a Year,	25	Foggy Night at Offord,	25
The Diamond Bracelet,	25	William Allair,	25
Clara Lake's Dream,	25	A Light and a Dark Christmas,	25
The Nobleman's Wife,	25	The Smuggler's Ghost,	25
Frances Hildyard,	25	Rupert Hall,	25
Cyrilla Maude's First Love,	25	My Husband's First Love,	25
My Cousin Caroline's Wedding	25	Marrying Beneath Your Station	25

EUGENE SUE'S GREAT WORKS.

The Wandering Jew,	$1 50	First Love,	50
The Mysteries of Paris,	1 50	Woman's Love,	50
Martin, the Foundling,	1 50	Female Bluebeard,	50
Above are in cloth at $2.00 each.		Man-of-War's-Man,	50
Life and Adventures of Raoul de Surville. A Tale of the Empire,			25

☞ Above Books will be sent, postage paid, on receipt of Retail Price, by T. B. Peterson & Brothers, Philadelphia, Pa.

MRS. HENRY WOOD'S BEST BOOKS, IN CLOTH.

The following are cloth editions of Mrs. Henry Wood's best books, and they are each issued in large octavo volumes, bound in cloth, price $1.75 each.

Within the Maze. By Mrs. Henry Wood, author of "East Lynne," $1 75
The Master of Greylands. By Mrs. Henry Wood, ... 1 75
Dene Hollow. By Mrs. Henry Wood, author of "Within the Maze," 1 75
Bessy Rane. By Mrs. Henry Wood, author of "The Channings,".... 1 75
George Canterbury's Will. By Mrs. Wood, author "Oswald Cray," 1 75
The Channings. By Mrs. Henry Wood, author of "Dene Hollow,"... 1 75
Roland Yorke. A Sequel to "The Channings." By Mrs. Wood,...... 1 75
Shadow of Ashlydyatt. By Mrs. Wood, author of "Bessy Rane,".... 1 75
Lord Oakburn's Daughters; or The Earl's Heirs. By Mrs. Wood,... 1 75
Verner's Pride. By Mrs. Henry Wood, author of "The Channings," 1 75
The Castle's Heir; or Lady Adelaide's Oath. By Mrs. Henry Wood, 1 75
Oswald Cray. By Mrs. Henry Wood, author of "Roland Yorke,".... 1 75
Squire Trevlyn's Heir; or Trevlyn Hold. By Mrs. Henry Wood,..... 1 75
The Red Court Farm. By Mrs. Wood, author of "Verner's Pride," 1 75
Elster's Folly. By Mrs. Henry Wood, author of "Castle's Heir,"... 1 75
St. Martin's Eve. By Mrs. Henry Wood, author of "Dene Hollow," 1 75
Mildred Arkell. By Mrs. Henry Wood, author of "East Lynne,".....1 75

WORKS BY THE VERY BEST AUTHORS.

The following books are each issued in one large duodecimo volume, bound in cloth, at $1.75 each, or each one is in paper cover, at $1.50 each.

The Initials. A Love Story. By Baroness Tautphœus,.................$1 75
Married Beneath Him. By author of "Lost Sir Massingberd,"...... 1 75
Margaret Maitland. By Mrs. Oliphant, author of "Zaidee,".......... 1 75
Family Pride. By author of "Pique," "Family Secrets," etc.......... 1 75
Self-Sacrifice. By author of "Margaret Maitland," etc................. 1 75
The Woman in Black. A Companion to the "Woman in White,"... 1 75
The Autobiography of Edward Wortley Montagu, ... 1 75
The Forsaken Daughter. A Companion to "Linda," 1 75
Love and Liberty. A Revolutionary Story. By Alexander Dumas, 1 75
The Morrisons. By Mrs. Margaret Hosmer,................................ 1 75
The Rich Husband. By author of "George Geith," 1 75
Woodburn Grange. A Novel. By William Howitt, ... 1 75
The Lost Beauty. By a Noted Lady of the Spanish Court,............. 1 75
My Hero. By Mrs. Forrester. A Charming Love Story,................ 1 75
The Quaker Soldier. A Revolutionary Romance. By Judge Jones,.... 1 75
Memoirs of Vidocq, the French Detective. His Life and Adventures, 1 75
The Belle of Washington. With her Portrait. By Mrs. N. P. Lasselle, 1 75
High Life in Washington. A Life Picture. By Mrs. N. P. Lasselle, 1 75
Above books are each in cloth, or each one is in paper cover, at $1.50 each.

☞ Above Books will be sent, postage paid, on Receipt of Retail Price, by T. B. Peterson & Brothers, Philadelphia, Pa.

8 T. B. PETERSON & BROTHERS' PUBLICATIONS.

WORKS BY THE VERY BEST AUTHORS.

The following books are each issued in one large duodecimo volume, bound in cloth, at $1.75 each, or each one is in paper cover at $1.50 each.

The Count of Monte-Cristo. By Alexander Dumas. Illustrated,...$1 75
The Countess of Monte-Cristo. Paper cover, price $1.00; or cloth,.. 1 75
Camille; or, the Fate of a Coquette. By Alexander Dumas,.......... 1 75
Love and Money. By J. B. Jones, author of the "Rival Belles,"... 1 75
The Brother's Secret; or, the Count De Mara. By William Godwin, 1 75
The Lost Love. By Mrs. Oliphant, author of "Margaret Maitland," 1 75
The Roman Traitor. By Henry William Herbert. A Roman Story, 1 75
The Bohemians of London. By Edward M. Whitty,................. 1 75
Wild Sports and Adventures in Africa. By Major W. C. Harris, 1 75
Courtship and Matrimony. By Robert Morris. With a Portrait,... 1 75
The Jealous Husband. By Annette Marie Maillard,............... 1 75
The Life, Writings, and Lectures of the late "Fanny Fern,"......... 1 75
The Life and Lectures of Lola Montez, with her portrait,........... 1 75
Wild Southern Scenes. By author of "Wild Western Scenes,"...... 1 75
Currer Lyle; or, the Autobiography of an Actress. By Louise Reeder. 1 75
The Cabin and Parlor. By J. Thornton Randolph. Illustrated,..... 1 75
The Little Beauty. A Love Story. By Mrs. Grey,.................. 1 75
Lizzie Glenn; or, the Trials of a Seamstress. By T. S. Arthur,..... 1 75
Lady Maud; or, the Wonder of Kingswood Chase. By Pierce Egan, 1 75
Wilfred Montressor; or, High Life in New York. Illustrated,....... 1 75
The Old Stone Mansion. By C. J. Peterson, author "Kate Aylesford," 1 75
Kate Aylesford. By Chas. J. Peterson, author "Old Stone Mansion,". 1 75
Lorrimer Littlegood, by author "Harry Coverdale's Courtship,"..... 1 75
The Earl's Secret. A Love Story. By Miss Pardoe,................ 1 75
The Adopted Heir. By Miss Pardoe, author of "The Earl's Secret," 1 75
Coal, Coal Oil, and all other Minerals in the Earth. By Eli Bowen, 1 75
Secession, Coercion, and Civil War. By J. B. Jones,............... 1 75

Above books are each in cloth, or each one is in paper cover, at $1.50 each.

The Dead Secret. By Wilkie Collins, author of "The Crossed Path," 1 50
The Crossed Path; or Basil. By Wilkie Collins,................... 1 50
Indiana. A Love Story. By George Sand, author of "Consuelo," 1 50
Jealousy; or, Teverino. By George Sand, author of "Consuelo," etc. 1 50
Six Nights with the Washingtonians, Illustrated. By T. S. Arthur, 3 50
Comstock's Elocution and Model Speaker. Intended for the use of
  Schools, Colleges, and for private Study, for the Promotion of
  Health, Cure of Stammering, and Defective Articulation. By
  Andrew Comstock and Philip Lawrence. With 236 Illustrations.. 2 00
The Lawrence Speaker. A Selection of Literary Gems in Poetry and
  Prose, designed for the use of Colleges, Schools, Seminaries, Literary
  Societies. By Philip Lawrence, Professor of Elocution. 600 pages.. 2 00

☞ **Above Books will be sent, postage paid, on receipt of Retail Price by T. B. Peterson & Brothers, Philadelphia, Pa.**

ALEXANDER DUMAS' WORKS, BOUND IN CLOTH.

The following are cloth editions of Dumas' and Reynolds' works, and they are each issued in large octavo volumes, bound in cloth, price $1.75 each.

The Three Guardsmen; or, The Three Mousquetaires. By A. Dumas, $1 75
Twenty Years After; or the "*Second Series of Three Guardsmen,*"... 1 75
Bragelonne; Son of Athos; or "*Third Series of Three Guardsmen,*" 1 75
The Iron Mask; or the "*Fourth Series of The Three Guardsmen,*".... 1 75
Louise La Valliere; or the "*Fifth Series and End of the Three Guardsmen Series,*"............ 1 75
The Memoirs of a Physician. By Alexander Dumas. Illustrated,... 1 75
Queen's Necklace; or "*Second Series of Memoirs of a Physician,*" 1 75
Six Years Later; or the "*Third Series of Memoirs of a Physician,*" 1 75
Countess of Charny; or "*Fourth Series of Memoirs of a Physician,*" 1 75
Andree De Taverney; or "*Fifth Series of Memoirs of a Physician,*" 1 75
The Chevalier; or the "*Sixth Series and End of the Memoirs of a Physician Series,*"............ 1 75
The Adventures of a Marquis. By Alexander Dumas,. 1 75
The Count of Monte-Cristo. By Alexander Dumas,................ 1 75
Edmond Dantes. A Sequel to the "Count of Monte-Cristo,".......... 1 75
The Forty-Five Guardsmen. By Alexander Dumas. Illustrated,... 1 75
Diana of Meridor, or Lady of Monsoreau. By Alexander Dumas,.... 1 75
The Iron Hand. By Alex. Dumas, author "Count of Monte-Cristo," 1 75
Camille; or the Fate of a Coquette. (La Dame aux Camelias,)...... 1 75
The Conscript. A novel of the Days of Napoleon the First,.......... 1 75
Love and Liberty. A novel of the French Revolution of 1792-1793, 1 75

GEORGE W. M. REYNOLDS' WORKS, IN CLOTH.

The Mysteries of the Court of London. By George W. M. Reynolds, 1 75
Rose Foster; or the "*Second Series of Mysteries of Court of London,*" 1 75
Caroline of Brunswick; or the "*Third Series of the Court of London,*" 1 75
Venetia Trelawney; or "*End of the Mysteries of the Court of London,*" 1 75
Lord Saxondale; or the Court of Queen Victoria. By Reynolds,...... 1 75
Count Christoval. Sequel to "Lord Saxondale." By Reynolds,....... 1 75
Rosa Lambert; or Memoirs of an Unfortunate Woman. By Reynolds, 1 75
Mary Price; or the Adventures of a Servant Maid. By Reynolds,... 1 75
Eustace Quentin. Sequel to "Mary Price." By G. W. M. Reynolds, 1 75
Joseph Wilmot; or the Memoirs of a Man Servant. By Reynolds,... 1 75
The Banker's Daughter. Sequel to "Joseph Wilmot." By Reynolds, 1 75
Kenneth. A Romance of the Highlands. By G. W. M. Reynolds, 1 75
Rye-House Plot; or the Conspirator's Daughter. By Reynolds,....... 1 75
Necromancer; or the Times of Henry the Eighth. By Reynolds,...... 1 75
The Mysteries of the Court of the Stuarts. By G. W. M. Reynolds, 1 75
Wallace; the Hero of Scotland. By G. W. M. Reynolds,............... 1 75
The Gipsy Chief. By George W. M. Reynolds,...................... 1 75
Robert Bruce; the Hero King of Scotland. By G. W. M. Reynolds, 1 75

☞ Above Books will be sent, postage paid, on receipt of Retail Price, by T. B. Peterson & Brothers, Philadelphia, Pa.

T. B. PETERSON & BROTHERS' PUBLICATIONS.

WORKS BY THE VERY BEST AUTHORS.

The following books are each issued in one large octavo volume, bound in cloth, at $2.00 each, or each one is done up in paper cover, at $1.50 each.

The Wandering Jew. By Eugene Sue. Full of Illustrations,	$2 00
Mysteries of Paris; and its Sequel, Gerolstein. By Eugene Sue,	2 00
Martin, the Foundling. By Eugene Sue. Full of Illustrations,	2 00
Ten Thousand a Year. By Samuel Warren. With Illustrations,	2 00
Washington and His Generals. By George Lippard,	2 00
The Quaker City; or, the Monks of Monk Hall. By George Lippard,	2 00
Blanche of Brandywine. By George Lippard,	2 00
Paul Ardenheim; the Monk of Wissahickon. By George Lippard,	2 00
The Mysteries of Florence. By Geo. Lippard, author "Quaker City,"	2 00
The Pictorial Tower of London. By W. Harrison Ainsworth,	2 50

Above books are each in cloth, or each one is in paper cover, at $1.50 each.

The following are each issued in one large octavo volume, bound in cloth, price $2.00 each, or a cheap edition is issued in paper cover, at 75 cents each.

Charles O'Malley, the Irish Dragoon. By Charles Lever, ...Cloth,	$2 00
Harry Lorrequer. With his Confessions. By Charles Lever,...Cloth,	2 00
Jack Hinton, the Guardsman. By Charles Lever, ...Cloth,	2 00
Davenport Dunn. A Man of Our Day. By Charles Lever,...Cloth,	2 00
Tom Burke of Ours. By Charles Lever, ...Cloth,	2 00
The Knight of Gwynne. By Charles Lever, ...Cloth,	2 00
Arthur O'Leary. By Charles Lever, ...Cloth,	2 00
Con Cregan. By Charles Lever, ...Cloth,	2 00
Horace Templeton. By Charles Lever, ...Cloth,	2 00
Kate O'Donoghue. By Charles Lever, ...Cloth,	2 00
Valentine Vox, the Ventriloquist. By Harry Cockton,......Cloth,	2 00

Above are each in cloth, or each one is in paper cover, at 75 cents each.

HUMOROUS ILLUSTRATED WORKS.

Each one is full of Illustrations, by Felix O. C. Darley, and bound in Cloth.

Major Jones' Courtship and Travels. With 21 Illustrations,	$1 75
Major Jones' Scenes in Georgia. With 16 Illustrations,	1 75
Simon Suggs' Adventures and Travels. With 17 Illustrations,	1 75
Swamp Doctor's Adventures in the South-West. 14 Illustrations,	1 50
Col. Thorpe's Scenes in Arkansaw. With 16 Illustrations,	1 50
The Big Bear's Adventures and Travels. With 18 Illustrations,	1 75
High Life in New York, by Jonathan Slick. With Illustrations,	1 75
Judge Haliburton's Yankee Stories. Illustrated,	1 75
Harry Coverdale's Courtship and Marriage. Illustrated,	1 75
Piney Wood's Tavern; or, Sam Slick in Texas. Illustrated,	1 75
Sam Slick, the Clockmaker. By Judge Haliburton. Illustrated,	1 75
Humors of Falconbridge. By J. F. Kelley. With Illustrations,	1 75
Modern Chivalry. By Judge Breckenridge. Two vols., each	1 75
Neal's Charcoal Sketches. By Joseph C. Neal. 21 Illustrations,	2 50

☞ Above Books will be sent, postage paid, on receipt of Retail Price, by T. B. Peterson & Brothers, Philadelphia, Pa.

NEW AND GOOD BOOKS BY BEST AUTHORS.

Beautiful Snow, and Other Poems. *New Illustrated Edition.* By J. W. Watson. With Illustrations by E. L. Henry. One volume, morocco cloth, black and gold, gilt top, side, and back, price $2.00; or in maroon morocco cloth, full gilt edges, full gilt back, full gilt sides, $3 00
The Outcast, and Other Poems. By J. W. Watson. One volume, green morocco cloth, gilt top, side and back, price $2.00; or in maroon morocco cloth, full gilt edges, full gilt back, full gilt sides,... 3 00
The Young Magdalen; and Other Poems. By Francis S. Smith, editor of "The New York Weekly." With a portrait of the author. Complete in one large volume of 300 pages, bound in green morocco cloth, gilt top, side, and back, price $3.00; or in full gilt,.... 4 00
Hans Breitmann's Ballads. By Charles G. Leland. *Containing the "First," "Second," "Third," "Fourth," and "Fifth Series" of Hans Breitmann's Ballads.* Complete in one large volume, bound in morocco cloth, gilt side, gilt top, and full gilt back, with beveled boards. With a full and complete Glossary to the whole work,..... 4 00
Meister Karl's Sketch Book. By Charles G. Leland. (Hans Breitmann.) Complete in one volume, green morocco cloth, gilt side, gilt top, gilt back, with beveled boards, price $2.50, or in maroon morocco cloth, full gilt edges, full gilt back, full gilt sides, etc.,........ 3 50
The Ladies' Guide to True Politeness and Perfect Manners. By Miss Leslie. Every lady should have it. Cloth, full gilt back,... 1 75
The Ladies' Complete Guide to Needlework and Embroidery. With 113 illustrations. By Miss Lambert. Cloth, full gilt back,......... 1 75
The Ladies' Work Table Book. With 27 illustrations. Cloth, gilt,. 1 50
Cyrilla; or the Mysterious Engagement. By author of "Initials," 1 00
The Miser's Daughter. By William Harrison Ainsworth, cloth,...... 1 75
John Jasper's Secret. A Sequel to Charles Dickens' "Mystery of Edwin Drood." With 18 Illustrations. Bound in cloth,............. 2 00
Across the Atlantic. Letters from France, Switzerland, Germany, Italy, and England. By C. H. Haeseler, M.D. Bound in cloth,... 2 00
Popery Exposed. An Exposition of Popery as it was and is, ... 1 75
The Story of Elizabeth. By Miss Thackeray, paper $1.00, or cloth,... 1 50
Dow's Short Patent Sermons. By Dow, Jr. In 4 vols., cloth, each.... 1 50
Wild Oats Sown Abroad. A Spicy Book. By T. B. Witmer, cloth,... 1 50
Aunt Patty's Scrap Bag. By Mrs. Caroline Lee Hentz. Illustrated, 1 50
Historical Sketches of Plymouth, Luzerne Co., Penna. By Hendrick B. Wright, of Wilkesbarre. With Twenty-five Photographs,...... 4 00

HARRY COCKTON'S BEST WORKS.

Valentine Vox, Ventriloquist,..	75	The Fatal Marriages,............	75
Valentine Vox, cloth,............	2 00	The Steward,.......................	75
Sylvester Sound, ...	75	Percy Effingham, ...	75
The Love Match, ...	75	The Prince,.........................	75

☞ Above Books will be sent, postage paid, on receipt of Retail Price, by T. B. Peterson & Brothers, Philadelphia, Pa.

12 T. B. PETERSON & BROTHERS' PUBLICATIONS.

NEW AND GOOD BOOKS BY BEST AUTHORS.

Consuelo. By George Sand. One volume, 12mo., bound in cloth,....$1 50
The Countess of Rudolstadt. Sequel to "Consuelo." 12mo., cloth,.. 1 50
Rose Foster. By George W. M. Reynolds, Esq., cloth,................. 1 75
Lord Montagu's Page. By G. P. R. James, author of "Cavalier,"... 1 75
Corinne; or, Italy. A Love Story. By Madame de Stael, cloth,.... 1 00
Treason at Home. A Novel. By Mrs. Greenough, cloth,............... 1 75
Letters from Europe. By Colonel John W. Forney. Bound in cloth, 1 75
Frank Fairlegh. By author of "Lewis Arundel," cloth,............... 1 75
Lewis Arundel. By author of "Frank Fairlegh," cloth,............... 1 75
Harry Racket Scapegrace. By the author of "Frank Fairlegh," cloth, 1 75
Tom Racquet. By author of "Frank Fairlegh," cloth,................. 1 75
La Gaviota; the Sea-Gull. By Fernan Caballero, cloth,............... 1 50
Monsieur Antoine. By George Sand. Illustrated. One vol., cloth, 1 00
Aurora Floyd. By Miss Braddon. One vol., paper 75 cents, cloth,... 1 00
The Life of Charles Dickens. By R. Shelton Mackenzie, cloth, ... 2 00
The Laws and Practice of the Game of Euchre, as adopted by the
  Euchre Club of Washington, D. C. Bound in cloth,................. 1 00
Poetical Works of Sir Walter Scott. One 8vo. volume, fine binding, 5 00
Life of Sir Walter Scott. By John G. Lockhart. With Portrait,...... 2 50
The Shakspeare Novels. Complete in one large octavo volume, cloth, 4 00
Miss Pardoe's Choice Novels. In one large octavo volume, cloth,... 4 00
Life, Speeches and Martyrdom of Abraham Lincoln. Illustrated,... 1 75
Rome and the Papacy. A History of the Men, Manners and Tempo-
  ral Government of Rome in the Nineteenth Century, cloth,......... 1 75
The French, German, Spanish, Latin and Italian Languages Without
  a Master. Whereby any one of these Languages can be learned
  without a Teacher. By A. H. Monteith. One volume, cloth,...... 2 00
Liebig's Complete Works on Chemistry. By Baron Justus Liebig... 2 00
Life and Adventures of Don Quixote and his Squire Sancho Panza, 1 75
Tan-go-ru-a. An Historical Drama, in Prose. By Mr. Moorhead,.... 1 00
The Impeachment Trial of President Andrew Johnson. Cloth,...... 1 50
Trial of the Assassins for the Murder of Abraham Lincoln. Cloth,... 1 50
Lives of Jack Sheppard and Guy Fawkes. Illustrated. One vol., cloth, 1 75
Christy and White's Complete Ethiopian Melodies, bound in cloth,... 1 00
Dr. Hollick's great work on the Anatomy and Physiology of the
  Human Figure, with colored dissected plates of the Human Figure, 2 00
Comstock's Colored Chart. Being a perfect Alphabet of the Eng-
  lish Language, Graphic and Typic, with exercises in Pitch, Force
  and Gesture, and Sixty-Eight colored figures, representing the va-
  rious postures and different attitudes to be used in declamation.
  On a large Roller. Every School should have a copy of it,......... 5 00
Riddell's Model Architect. With 22 large full page colored illustrations, and 44 plates of ground plans, with plans, specifications,
  costs of building, etc. One large quarto volume, bound,............ 15 00

☞ Above Books will be sent, postage paid, on receipt of Retail Price, by T. B. Peterson & Brothers, Philadelphia, Pa.

WORKS BY THE VERY BEST AUTHORS.

The Conscript; or, the Days of Napoleon 1st. By Alex. Dumas,.....$1 75
Cousin Harry. By Mrs. Grey, author of "The Gambler's Wife," etc. 1 75
Married at Last. A Love Story. By Annie Thomas,..................... 1 75
Shoulder Straps. By Henry Morford, author of "Days of Shoddy," 1 75
Days of Shoddy. By Henry Morford, author of "Shoulder Straps," 1 75
The Coward. By Henry Morford, author of "Shoulder Straps,"..... 1 75
  Above books are each in cloth, or each one is in paper cover, at $1.50 each.

Harry Lorrequer. *With His Confessions.* By Charles Lever. *Four different editions:* one at 75 cents in paper cover, and three bound in cloth, viz.: Sterling Series, at $1.00, Peoples' Edition, at $1.50, and Library Edition, at $2.00.

Charles O'Malley, the Irish Dragoon. *Four different editions:* one at 75 cents in paper cover, and three bound in cloth, viz.: Sterling Series, at $1.00, Peoples' Edition, at $1.50, and Library Edition, at $2.00.

WORKS IN SETS BY THE BEST AUTHORS.

Mrs. Emma D. E. N. Southworth's Popular Novels. 43 vols. in all, 75 25
Mrs. Ann S. Stephens' Celebrated Novels. 23 volumes in all,......... 40 25
Miss Eliza A. Dupuy's Works. Fourteen volumes in all,............... 24 50
Mrs. Caroline Lee Hentz's Novels. Twelve volumes in all,............ 21 00
Mrs. C. A. Warfield's Novels. Nine volumes in all,....................... 15 75
Frederika Bremer's Novels. Six volumes in all,........................... 10 50
T. Adolphus Trollope's Works. Seven volumes in all,.................. 12 25
James A. Maitland's Novels. Seven volumes in all,...................... 12 25
Charles Lever's Works. Ten volumes in all,................................ 20 00
Alexander Dumas' Works. Twenty-one volumes in all, ... 36 75
George W. M. Reynolds' Works. Eighteen volumes in all,........... 31 50
Frank Fairlegh's Works. Six volumes in all,............................... 10 50
Q. K. Philander Doesticks's Novels. Four volumes in all,............ 7 00
Cook Books. The best in the world. Eleven volumes in all,........ 19 25
Henry Morford's Novels. Three volumes in all,.......................... 5 25
Mrs. Henry Wood's Novels. Seventeen volumes in all,................. 29 75
Emerson Bennett's Novels. Seven volumes in all,....................... 12 25
Green's Works on Gambling. Four volumes in all,..................... 7 00
American Humorous Works. Illustrated. Twelve volumes in all, 21 00
Eugene Sue's Best Works. Three volumes in all,....................... 6 00
George Sand's Works. Consuelo, etc. Five volumes in all,......... 7 50
George Lippard's Works. Five volumes in all,........................... 10 00
Dow's Short Patent Sermons. Four volumes in all,..................... 6 00
The Waverley Novels. *National Edition.* Five large 8vo. vols., cloth, 15 00
Charles Dickens' Works. *People's 12mo. Edition.* 22 vols., cloth, 34 00
Charles Dickens' Works. *Green Cloth 12mo. Edition.* 22 vols., cloth, 44 00
Charles Dickens' Works. *Illustrated 12mo. Edition.* 36 vols., cloth, 55 00
Charles Dickens' Works. *Illustrated 8vo. Edition.* 18 vols., cloth, 31 50
Charles Dickens' Works. *New National Edition.* 7 volumes, cloth, 20 00

☞ Above Books will be sent, postage paid, on receipt of Retail Price, by T. B. Peterson & Brothers, Philadelphia, Pa.

CHARLES DICKENS' WORKS.

☞ GREAT REDUCTION IN THEIR PRICES. ☜

CHEAP PAPER COVER EDITION OF DICKENS' WORKS.
Each book being complete in one large octavo volume.

Pickwick Papers,	50	Bleak House,	50
Nicholas Nickleby,	50	Little Dorrit,	50
Dombey and Son,	50	Christmas Stories,	50
Our Mutual Friend,	50	Barnaby Rudge,	50
David Copperfield,	50	Sketches by "Boz,"	50
Martin Chuzzlewit,	50	Great Expectations,	50
Old Curiosity Shop,	50	Joseph Grimaldi,	50
Oliver Twist,	50	The Pic-Nic Papers,	50
American Notes,	25	The Haunted House,	25
Hard Times,	25	Uncommercial Traveller,	25
A Tale of Two Cities,	25	A House to Let,	25
Somebody's Luggage,	25	Perils of English Prisoners,	25
Mrs. Lirriper's Lodgings,	25	Wreck of the Golden Mary,	25
Mrs. Lirriper's Legacy,	25	Tom Tiddler's Ground,	25
Mugby Junction,	25	Dickens' New Stories,	25
Dr. Marigold's Prescriptions,	25	Lazy Tour of Idle Apprentices,	25
Mystery of Edwin Drood,	25	The Holly-Tree Inn,	25
Message from the Sea,	25	No Thoroughfare,	25
Hunted Down; and Other Reprinted Pieces,			50

PEOPLE'S DUODECIMO EDITION. ILLUSTRATED.
Reduced in price from $2.50 to $1.50 a volume.
This edition is printed on fine paper, from large, clear type, leaded, that all can read, containing Two Hundred Illustrations on tinted paper.

Our Mutual Friend, Cloth,	$1.50	Little Dorrit, Cloth,	$1.50
Pickwick Papers, Cloth,	1.50	Dombey and Son, Cloth,	1.50
Nicholas Nickleby, Cloth,	1.50	Christmas Stories, Cloth,	1.50
Great Expectations, Cloth,	1.50	Sketches by "Boz," Cloth,	1.50
David Copperfield, Cloth,	1.50	Barnaby Rudge, Cloth,	1.50
Oliver Twist, Cloth,	1.50	Martin Chuzzlewit, Cloth,	1.50
Bleak House, Cloth,	1.50	Old Curiosity Shop, Cloth,	1.50
A Tale of Two Cities, Cloth,	1.50	Dickens' New Stories, Cloth,	1.50

Mystery of Edwin Drood; and Master Humphrey's Clock, Cloth, 1.50
American Notes; and the Uncommercial Traveller, Cloth, 1.50
Hunted Down; and other Reprinted Pieces, Cloth, 1.50
The Holly-Tree Inn; and other Stories, Cloth, 1.50
The Life and Writings of Charles Dickens, Cloth, 2.00
John Jasper's Secret. Sequel to Mystery of Edwin Drood, Cloth, 2.00
Price of a set, in Black cloth, in twenty-two volumes, $34.00
" " Full sheep, Library style, 45.00
" " Half calf, sprinkled edges, 56.00
" " Half calf, marbled edges, 61.00
" " Half calf, antique, or half calf, full gilt backs, etc. 66.00

☞ Above Books will be sent, postage paid, on receipt of Retail Price, by T. B. Peterson & Brothers, Philadelphia, Pa.

HUMOROUS AMERICAN WORKS.

With Illuminated Covers, and beautifully Illustrated by Felix O. C. Darley.

Major Jones's Courtship. With Illustrations by Darley,	75
Major Jones's Sketches of Travels. Full of Illustrations	75
The Adventures of Captain Simon Suggs. Illustrated,	75
Major Jones's Chronicles of Pineville. Illustrated,	75
Polly Peablossom's Wedding. With Illustrations,	75
Widow Rugby's Husband. Full of Illustrations,	75
The Big Bear of Arkansas. Illustrated by Darley,	75
Western Scenes; or, Life on the Prairie. Illustrated,	75
Streaks of Squatter Life and Far West Scenes. Illustrated,	75
Pickings from the New Orleans Picayune. Illustrated,	75
Stray Subjects Arrested and Bound Over. Illustrated,	75
The Louisiana Swamp Doctor. Full of Illustrations,	75
Charcoal Sketches. By Joseph C. Neal. Illustrated,	75
Peter Faber's Misfortunes. By Joseph C. Neal. Illustrated,	75
Peter Ploddy and other Oddities. By Joseph C. Neal,	75
Yankee Among the Mermaids. By William E. Burton.	75
The Drama in Pokerville. By J. M. Field. Illustrated,	75
New Orleans Sketch Book. With Illustrations by Darley,	75
The Deer Stalkers. By Frank Forrester. Illustrated,	75
The Quorndon Hounds. By Frank Forrester. Illustrated,	75
My Shooting Box. By Frank Forrester. Illustrated,	75
The Warwick Woodlands. By Frank Forrester. Illustrated,	75
Adventures of Captain Farrago. By H. H. Brackenridge,	75
Adventures of Major O'Regan. By H. H. Brackenridge,	75
Sol Smith's Theatrical Apprenticeship. Illustrated,	75
Sol Smith's Theatrical Journey-Work. Illustrated,	75
Quarter Race in Kentucky. With Illustrations by Darley,	75
The Mysteries of the Backwoods. By T. B. Thorpe,	75
Percival Mayberry's Adventures. By J. H. Ingraham,	75
Sam Slick's Yankee Yarns and Yankee Letters,	75
Adventures of Fudge Fumble; or, Love Scrapes of his Life,	75
Aunt Patty's Scrap Bag. By Mrs. Caroline Lee Hentz,	75
Following the Drum. By Mrs. Gen. Viele,	50
The American Joe Miller. With 100 Engravings,	50

SAMUEL WARREN'S BEST BOOKS.

Ten Thousand a Year, paper,	$1 50
Ten Thousand a Year, cloth,	2 00
The Diary of a Medical Student,	75

WILLIAM H. MAXWELL'S WORKS.

Wild Sports of the West,	75	Brian O'Lynn,	75
Stories of Waterloo,	75	Life of Grace O'Malley,	50

☞ Above Books will be sent, postage paid, on receipt of Retail Price, by T. B. Peterson & Brothers, Philadelphia, Pa.

NEW BOOKS BY THE BEST AUTHORS.
FOR SALE BY ALL BOOKSELLERS, AND PUBLISHED BY
T. B. PETERSON & BROTHERS, PHILADELPHIA.

L'ASSOMMOIR. *A Novel. By Emile Zola,* author of "The Rougon-Macquart Family," "Helene," etc. Price 75 cents in paper cover, or $1.00 in cloth.

THE ROUGON-MACQUART FAMILY; or, LA FORTUNE DES ROUGON. *By Emile Zola,* author of "L'Assommoir." Price 75 cents in paper, or $1.25 in cloth.

HELENE, A LOVE EPISODE; or, UNE PAGE D'AMOUR. *By Emile Zola,* author of "L'Assommoir," etc. Price 75 cents in paper cover, or $1.25 in cloth.

THE ABBE'S TEMPTATION; or, LA FAUTE DE L'ABBE MOURET. *By Emile Zola,* author of "L'Assommoir." Price 75 cents in paper cover, or $1.25 in cloth.

UNDER THE WILLOWS; or, THE THREE COUNTESSES. *By Elizabeth Van Loon,* author of "A Heart Twice Won," "Shadow of Hampton Mead." Cloth, $1.50.

MARKOF, THE RUSSIAN VIOLINIST. *A Russian Story. By Henry Greville,* author of "Dosia." One large volume, cloth, price $1.50, or 75 cents in paper cover.

MAJOR JONES'S COURTSHIP. Author's New Edition. *By Major Joseph Jones,* of Pineville, Georgia. With 21 Illustrations by Darley and Cary. Price 75 cents.

A HEART TWICE WON; or, SECOND LOVE. *A Love Story. By Mrs. Elizabeth Van Loon,* author of "The Shadow of Hampton Mead." Cloth, price $1.50.

THE SHADOW OF HAMPTON MEAD. *A Charming Story. By Mrs. Elizabeth Van Loon,* author of "A Heart Twice Won." Cloth, black and gold. Price $1.50.

DOSIA. *A Russian Story. By Henry Gréville,* author of "Marrying Off a Daughter," "Savéli's Expiation," and "Gabrielle." Price 75 cents in paper, or $1.25 in cloth.

MAJOR JONES'S SCENES IN GEORGIA. With Full Page Illustrations, from Original Designs by Darley. Morocco cloth, gilt and black. Price $1.50.

THE LAST ATHENIAN. *By Victor Rydberg.* This is one of the most remarkable books ever published. One volume, 12mo., 600 pages, cloth, price $1.75.

MARRYING OFF A DAUGHTER. *A Love Story. By Henry Gréville,* author of "Dosia," "Savéli's Expiation," and "Markof." Price 75 cts. in paper, or $1.25 in cloth.

PHILOMENE'S MARRIAGES. With Author's Preface. *By Henry Gréville,* author of "Dosia." Price 75 cents in paper cover, or $1.25 in cloth.

PRETTY LITTLE COUNTESS ZINA. *By Henry Gréville,* author of "Dosia," "Savéli's Expiation," and "Markof." Price 75 cents in paper, or $1.25 in cloth.

THE COUNT DE CAMORS. *The Man of the Second Empire. By Octave Feuillet,* author of "The Amours of Phillippe." Price 75 cents in paper, or $1.25 in cloth.

THE SWAMP DOCTOR'S ADVENTURES IN THE SOUTH-WEST. With Fourteen Illustrations, from Designs by Darley. Morocco cloth, gilt and black. Price $1.50.

COLONEL THORPE'S SCENES IN ARKANSAW. With Sixteen Illustrations, from Original Designs by Darley. Morocco cloth, gilt and black. Price $1.50.

HIGH LIFE IN NEW YORK. By Jonathan Slick. Illustrated. Price $1.50.

RANCY COTTEM'S COURTSHIP. By author "Major Jones's Courtship." 50 cts.

JARL'S DAUGHTER. *By Mrs. Frances Hodgson Burnett.* Paper, price 25 cents.

LINDSAY'S LUCK. *By Mrs. Frances Hodgson Burnett.* Paper, price 25 cents.

☞ *Above Books are for sale by all Booksellers and News Agents, or copies of any one or all of them, will be sent to any one, post-paid, on remitting price to the Publishers,*

T. B. PETERSON & BROTHERS, Philadelphia, Pa.

NEW BOOKS BY THE BEST AUTHORS.

Price 50 Cents each in paper cover, or $1.00 each in cloth.

BONNE-MARIE. A Love Story. *By Henry Gréville,* author of "Dosia," "Marrying Off a Daughter," "Savéli's Expiation," "Markof," and "Gabrielle."
MISS MARGERY'S ROSES. A Charming Love Story. *By Robert C. Meyers.*
DOURNOF. A Russian Story. *By Henry Gréville,* author of "Dosia," "Savéli's Expiation," "Bonne-Marie," and "Marrying Off a Daughter."
"THEO." A Love Story. *By Mrs. Burnett,* author of "Kathleen."
KATHLEEN. A Love Story. *By Mrs. Frances Hodgson Burnett,* author of "Theo," "Pretty Polly Pemberton," "Miss Crespigny," "A Quiet Life," etc.
MISS CRESPIGNY. A Love Story. *By Mrs. Burnett,* author of "Theo."
SONIA. A Russian Love Story. *By Henry Gréville,* author of "Marrying Off a Daughter," "Dosia," "Markof," etc. *Translated by Mary Neal Sherwood.*
A QUIET LIFE. *By Mrs. Burnett,* author of "Kathleen," and "Theo."
A FRIEND; or, L'AMIE. *By Henry Gréville,* author of "Sonia," "Savéli's Expiation," "Markof," and "Marrying Off a Daughter."
PRETTY POLLY PEMBERTON. A Love Story. *By Mrs. Burnett.*
A WOMAN'S MISTAKE; or, JACQUES DE TREVANNES. A Charming Love Story. *By Madame Angèle Dussaud. Translated by Mary Neal Sherwood.*
SYBIL BROTHERTON. A Novel. *By Mrs. Emma D. E. N. Southworth.*
FATHER TOM AND THE POPE; or, A NIGHT AT THE VATICAN. With Illustrations of the scenes that took place between the Pope and Father Tom.
MADELEINE. A Love Story. *By Jules Sandeau.* Crowned by French Academy.
SAVELI'S EXPIATION. *By Henry Gréville,* author of "Dosia." A dramatic and powerful novel of Russian life. *Translated by Mary Neal Sherwood.*
TWO WAYS TO MATRIMONY; or, IS IT LOVE? or, FALSE PRIDE.
GABRIELLE; or, THE HOUSE OF MAUREZE. *Translated from the French of Henry Gréville,* author of "Savéli's Expiation," "Markof," "Sonia," "Dosia."
STORY OF "ELIZABETH." *By Miss Thackeray,* daughter of W. M. Thackeray.
THE DAYS OF MADAME POMPADOUR; or, MADAME POMPADOUR'S GARTER. A Romance of the Reign of Louis XV. *By Gabrielle D. St. Andre.*
CARMEN. *By Prosper Mérimee.* From which opera of "Carmen" was dramatized.
THE MATCHMAKER. A Charming Novel. *By Beatrice Reynolds.* All the characters and scenes in it, have all the freshness of life, and vitality of truth.
THE RED HILL TRAGEDY. *By Mrs. Emma D. E. N. Southworth.*
THE AMOURS OF PHILLIPPE. "PHILLIPPE'S LOVE AFFAIRS." *By Feuillet.*
FANCHON, THE CRICKET; or, LA PETITE FADETTE. *By George Sand.*
BESSIE'S SIX LOVERS. A Charming Love Story, of the purest and best kind.
THAT GIRL OF MINE. A Love Story. By the author of *"That Lover of Mine."*
THAT LOVER OF MINE. By the author of *"That Girl of Mine."*

Above are 50 Cents each in paper cover, or $1.00 each in cloth.

☞ *Above Books are for sale by all Booksellers and News Agents, or copies of any one or all of them, will be sent to any one, post-paid, on remitting price to the publishers,*

T. B. PETERSON & BROTHERS, Philadelphia, Pa.

HOW SHE WON HIM!
OR,
THE BRIDE OF CHARMING VALLEY.
BY DAVID A. MOORE.

"HOW SHE WON HIM; OR, THE BRIDE OF CHARMING VALLEY," might more properly be called "a realistic romance" than a novel, for every incident in it—and many of them are wild and wonderful to a degree—*might* have happened. The hero of this story starts for the West, while yet in his teens, leaving his home in a Pennsylvanian village, and, with his mother, settles down in Cincinnati, where he has the good fortune to win the favor of a liberal-minded banker, who gives him employment, and to whom, in the fulness of time, he is able in turn to render essential service. When he attains manhood, he follows Bacon's advice, of giving hostages to fortune by taking a wife—not, however, his first love. There is a little mystery here, which the reader will find cleared up very satisfactorily in the end. Leon Gaylord, having a passion for adventure, and a conviction that enterprise, perseverance, and good conduct cannot fail to win success, goes to the Pacific coast, soon after the wondrous resources of California had begun to be developed, leaving his mother and wife in Cincinnati, and, though not without trouble from the Indians, who regarded all gold-hunters as interlopers, eventually becomes very rich, and even obtains a seat on the bench in a district in California, whence he dispenses justice to the satisfaction of all except criminals. At last, still a young man, for he had begun life early, he returns to the East with the large fortune he had realized. His wife had died, years before, leaving a son. The wealth laboriously and honestly obtained is judiciously and liberally dispensed—but the romance of his life may be said to begin again at Saratoga, the end being a second marriage, with the happiest auspices and under very strange circumstances. The numerous characters in this life-drama are so cleverly sketched that it seems as if they were pen-photographs—if such things are.—CRITIC.

Paper Cover, 50 Cents. Morocco Cloth, Gilt and Black, $1.00.

☞ "*How She Won Him*" is printed on tinted paper, and is issued in square 12mo. form, in uniform shape with "*L'Assommoir,*" "*Hélène; a Love Episode,*" or, "*Une Page d'Amour,*" "*The Abbé's Temptation,*" "*The Conquest of Plassans,*" "*The Rougon-Macquart Family;*" or, "*La Fortune Des Rougon,*" "*The Markets of Paris,*" and other works of Emile Zola's published by us, and is for sale by all Booksellers, or copies will be sent to any one, at once, post-paid, on remitting price to the Publishers,

T. B. PETERSON & BROTHERS,
306 Chestnut Street, Philadelphia, Pa.

NEW BOOKS BY THE BEST AUTHORS.

FOR SALE BY ALL BOOKSELLERS, AND PUBLISHED BY

T. B. PETERSON & BROTHERS, PHILADELPHIA.

HIS EXCELLENCY EUGENE ROUGON. *By Emile Zola*, author of "L'Assommoir," "Nana," "Helene," etc. Price 75 cents in paper, or $1.25 in cloth.

MYRTLE LAWN. A New American Novel. *By Robert E. Ballard*, of North Carolina. The dialogues and correspondence in this tale are admirable, and the author's stream of narrative is at once clear, strong and rapid, including a spirited sketch of the Carlist war in Spain, in which, at the storming of a stronghold, success is unexpectedly and brilliantly achieved by the self-devoted valor of the hero, a dashing young American. It is a panoramic painting in words, such as Scott or Macaulay might have dashed off in a happy hour of literary excitement. There is nothing of the sort finer in modern fiction. Cloth, black and gold. Price $1.50.

THE MARKETS OF PARIS; or, LE VENTRE DE PARIS. *By Emile Zola*, author of "L'Assommoir," "Nana," etc. Price 75 cents in paper, or $1.25 in cloth.

HYDE PARK SKETCHES. By *A. Western*. The author of "Hyde Park Sketches" used his eyes to observe, his ears to listen, his voice to inquire, his memory to retain, and his pen to record all that he had learned about the highways and byeways of the greatest city on earth. Original characters are described with vivid force, eccentric persons are brought forward, and nothing dull appears in the sketches, in which the "West End" of mighty London is made to pass before us, as in review. Price 50 cents in paper cover, or $1.00 in cloth.

THE CONQUEST OF PLASSANS; or, LA CONQUETE DE PLASSANS. *By Emile Zola*, author of "L'Assommoir," "Nana." Price 75 cents in paper, or $1.25 in cloth.

THE OLD STONE MANSION. An American Novel, by an American Author. This is one of the most thrilling, powerful, and absorbing romances of real life ever penned. It is full of stirring incidents and strongly drawn scenes, is intensely interesting on every page, yet so beautiful in style, and so true to nature, that it can be read with delight by all. Cloth, black and gold. Price $1.50.

ANGELE'S FORTUNE. A Story of Real Life. *By Andre Theuriet*. His New and Best Work. Translated and Adapted from the French by Mary Neal Sherwood. Price 75 cents in paper cover, or $1.25 in cloth.

COURTSHIP AND MATRIMONY. With Other Sketches from Scenes and Experiences in Social Life, adapted for Every-day Reading by all classes of Society. *By Robert Morris*, editor of the Philadelphia Inquirer, with a Steel-plate Portrait of the Author. One large duodecimo volume, morocco cloth, black and gold, price $1.50.

THE EARL OF MAYFIELD. *A New Novel. By a Southerner.* Fifth Edition Now Ready. Great success of it. Everybody is reading and recommending it. Complete in one large duodecimo volume, morocco cloth, black and gold, price $1.50.

ST. MAUR; AN EARL'S WOOING. A New Society Novel. *By John Carroll*, "Caves," Baltimore Co., Md. Price 75 cents in paper, or $1.25 in cloth.

HOW SHE WON HIM; or, THE BRIDE OF CHARMING VALLEY. *By D. A. Moore*. The numerous characters in this life-drama are so cleverly sketched that it seems as if they were pen-photographs. Price 75 cents in paper cover, or $1.25 in cloth.

☞ *Above Books are for sale by all Booksellers and News Agents, or copies of any one or all of them, will be sent to any one, post-paid, on remitting price to the Publishers,*

T. B. PETERSON & BROTHERS, Philadelphia, Pa.

PETERSONS' DOLLAR SERIES

OF GOOD AND NEW NOVELS, ARE THE BEST, LARGEST, AND
CHEAPEST BOOKS IN THE WORLD.
Price One Dollar Each, in Cloth, Black and Gold.

A WOMAN'S THOUGHTS ABOUT WOMEN. By Miss Mulock. Every Lady wants it.
TWO WAYS TO MATRIMONY; or, Is It Love, or, False Pride?
THE STORY OF "ELIZABETH." By Miss Thackeray, daughter of W. M. Thackeray.
FLIRTATIONS IN FASHIONABLE LIFE. By Catharine Sinclair.
THE MATCHMAKER. A Society Novel. By Beatrice Reynolds. Full of freshness and truth.
ROSE DOUGLAS, The Bonnie Scotch Lass. A companion to "Family Pride."
THE EARL'S SECRET. A Charming and Sentimental Love Story. By Miss Pardoe.
FAMILY SECRETS. A companion to "Family Pride," and a very fascinating work.
A LONELY LIFE. A Thrilling Novel in Real Life.
THE MACDERMOTS OF BALLYCLORAN. An Exciting Novel by Anthony Trollope.
THE FAMILY SAVE-ALL. With Economical Receipts for Breakfast, Dinner and Tea.
SELF-SACRIFICE. A Charming and Exciting work. By author of "Margaret Maitland."
THE PRIDE OF LIFE. A Love Story. By Lady Jane Scott.
THE RIVAL BELLES; or, Life in Washington. By author "Wild Western Scenes."
THE CLYFFARDS OF CLYFFE. By James Payn, author of "Lost Sir Massingberd."
THE ORPHAN'S TRIALS; or, Alone in a Great City. By Emerson Bennett.
THE HEIRESS OF SWEETWATER. A Love Story, abounding with exciting scenes.
THE REFUGEE. A delightful book, full of food for laughter, and sterling information.
LOST SIR MASSINGBERD. A Love Story. By author of "The Clyffards of Clyffe."
CORA BELMONT; or, THE SINCERE LOVER. A True Story of the Heart.
THE LOVER'S TRIALS; or, The Days Before the Revolution. By Mrs. Denison.
MY SON'S WIFE. A strong, bright, interesting, and charming Novel. By author of "Caste."
AUNT PATTY'S SCRAP BAG. By Mrs. Caroline Lee Hentz, author of "Linda," "Rena."
SARATOGA! AND THE FAMOUS SPRINGS. An Indian Tale of Frontier Life.
COUNTRY QUARTERS. A Charming Love Story. By the Countess of Blessington.
SELF-LOVE. A Book for Young Ladies, with their prospects in Single and Married Life contrasted.
LOVE AND DUTY. A Charming Love Story. By Mrs. Hubback.
THE DEVOTED BRIDE; or, FAITH AND FIDELITY. A Love Story.
THE HEIRESS IN THE FAMILY. By author of "Marrying for Money."
COLLEY CIBBER'S LIFE OF EDWIN FORREST, with Reminiscences.
THE MAN OF THE WORLD. This is full of style, elegance of diction, and force of thought.
OUT OF THE DEPTHS. A Woman's Story and a Woman's book, the Story of a Woman's Life.
THE QUEEN'S FAVORITE; or, The Price of a Crown. A Romance of Don Juan.
THE CAVALIER. A Novel. By G. P. R. James, author of "Lord Montagu's Page."
THE RECTOR'S WIFE; or, THE VALLEY OF A HUNDRED FIRES.
THE COQUETTE; or, LIFE AND LETTERS OF ELIZA WHARTON.
WOMAN'S WRONG. A Book for Women. By Mrs. Elloart. A Novel of great power.
HAREM LIFE IN EGYPT AND CONSTANTINOPLE. By Emmeline Lott.
THE OLD PATROON; or, The GREAT VAN BROEK PROPERTY.
THE BEAUTIFUL WIDOW. **TREASON AT HOME.** **PANOLA!**

☞ *The above Books are all issued in "Petersons' Dollar Series," and they will be found for sale by all Booksellers, News Agents, and on all Railroad trains, at One Dollar each, or copies of any one, or more, will be sent to any place, at once, post-paid, on remitting the price of the ones wanted in a letter, to*

T. B. PETERSON & BROTHERS, Philadelphia.

GEORGE W. M. REYNOLDS' WORKS.
NEW AND BEAUTIFUL EDITIONS, JUST READY.

Each Work is complete and unabridged, in one large volume.

All or any will be sent free of postage, everywhere, to all, on receipt of remittances.

Mysteries of the Court of London; *being* THE MYSTERIES OF THE COURT OF GEORGE THE THIRD, *with the Life and Times of the* PRINCE OF WALES, *afterward* GEORGE THE FOURTH. Complete in one large volume, bound in cloth, price $1.75; or in paper cover, price $1.00.
Rose Foster; or, the "Second Series of the Mysteries of the Court of London." Complete in one large volume, bound in cloth, price $1.75; or in paper cover, price $1.50.
Caroline of Brunswick; or, the "Third Series of the Mysteries of the Court of London." Complete in one large volume, bound in cloth, price $1.75; or in paper cover, price $1.00.
Venetia Trelawney; being the "Fourth Series or final conclusion of the Mysteries of the Court of London." Complete in one large volume, bound in cloth, price $1.75; or in paper cover, price $1.00.
Lord Saxondale; or, The Court of Queen Victoria. Complete in one large volume, bound in cloth, price $1.75; or in paper cover, price $1.00.
Count Christoval. The "Sequel to Lord Saxondale." Complete in one large volume, bound in cloth, price $1.75; or in paper cover, price $1.00.
Rosa Lambert; or, The Memoirs of an Unfortunate Woman. Complete in one large volume, bound in cloth, price $1.75; or in paper cover, price $1.00.
Joseph Wilmot; or, The Memoirs of a Man Servant. Complete in one large volume, bound in cloth, price $1.75; or in paper cover, price $1.00.
The Banker's Daughter. A Sequel to "Joseph Wilmot." Complete in one large volume, bound in cloth, price $1.75; or in paper cover, price $1.00.
The Rye-House Plot; or, Ruth, the Conspirator's Daughter. Complete in one large volume, bound in cloth, price $1.75; or in paper cover, price $1.00.
The Necromancer. Being the Mysteries of the Court of Henry the Eighth. Complete in one large volume, bound in cloth, price $1.75; or in paper cover, price $1.00.
Mary Price; or, The Adventures of a Servant Maid. One vol., cloth, price $1.75; or in paper. $1.00
Eustace Quentin. A "Sequel to Mary Price." One vol., cloth, price $1.75; or in paper, $1.00.
The Mysteries of the Court of Naples. Price $1.00 in paper cover; or $1.75 in cloth.
Kenneth. A Romance of the Highlands. One vol., cloth, price $1.75; or in paper cover, $1.00.
Wallace: the Hero of Scotland. Illustrated with 38 plates. Paper, $1.00; cloth, $1.75.
The Gipsy Chief. Beautifully Illustrated. Price $1.00 in paper cover, or $1.75 in cloth.
Robert Bruce; the Hero King of Scotland. Illustrated. Paper, $1.00; cloth, $1.75.
The Opera Dancer; or, The Mysteries of London Life. Price 75 cents.
Isabella Vincent; or, The Two Orphans. One large octavo volume. Price 75 cents.
Vivian Bertram; or, A Wife's Honor. A Sequel to "Isabella Vincent." Price 75 cents.
The Countess of Lascelles. The Continuation to "Vivian Bertram." Price 75 cents.
Duke of Marchmont. Being the Conclusion of "The Countess of Lascelles." Price 75 cents.
The Child of Waterloo; or, The Horrors of the Battle Field. Price 75 cents.
Pickwick Abroad. A Companion to the "Pickwick Papers," by "Boz." Price 75 cents.
The Countess and the Page. One large octavo volume. Price 75 cents.
Mary Stuart, Queen of Scots. Complete in one large octavo volume. Price 75 cents.
The Soldier's Wife. Illustrated. One large octavo volume. Price 75 cents.
May Middleton; or, The History of a Fortune. In one large octavo volume. Price 75 cents.
The Loves of the Harem. One large octavo volume. Price 75 cents.
Ellen Percy; or, The Memoirs of an Actress. One large octavo volume. Price 75 cents.
The Discarded Queen. One large octavo volume. Price 75 cents.
Agnes Evelyn; or, Beauty and Pleasure. One large octavo volume. Price 75 cents.
The Massacre of Glencoe. One large octavo volume. Price 75 cents.
The Parricide; or, Youth's Career in Crime. Beautifully Illustrated. Price 75 cents.
Ciprina; or, The Secrets of a Picture Gallery. One volume. Price 50 cents.
The Ruined Gamester. With Illustrations. One large octavo volume. Price 50 cents.
Life in Paris. Handsomely illustrated. One large octavo volume. Price 50 cents.
Clifford and the Actress. One large octavo volume. Price 50 cents.
Edgar Montrose. One large octavo volume. Price 50 cents.

☞ *The above works will be found for sale by all Booksellers and News Agents.*

☞ *Copies of any one, or more, or all of Reynolds' works, will be sent to any place at once, post-paid, on remitting price of ones wanted to the Publishers,*

T. B. PETERSON & BROTHERS, Philadelphia, Pa.

ALEXANDER DUMAS' GREAT WORKS.

All or any will be sent free of postage, everywhere, to all, on receipt of remittances.

The Count of Monte-Cristo. With elegant illustrations, and portraits of Edmond Dantes, Mercedes, and Fernand. Price $1.50 in paper cover; or $1.75 in cloth.
Edmond Dantes. A Sequel to the "Count of Monte-Cristo." In one large octavo volume. Price 75 cents in paper cover, or a finer edition, bound in cloth, for $1.75.
The Countess of Monte-Cristo. With a portrait of the "Countess of Monte-Cristo" on the cover. One large octavo volume, paper cover, price $1.00; or bound in cloth, for $1.75.
The Three Guardsmen; or, The Three Mousquetaires. In one large octavo volume. Price 75 cents in paper cover, or a finer edition in cloth, for $1.75.
Twenty Years After. A Sequel to the "Three Guardsmen." In one large octavo volume. Price 75 cents in paper cover, or a finer edition, in one volume, cloth, for $1.75.
Bragelonne; the Son of Athos. Being the continuation of "Twenty Years After." In one large octavo volume. Price 75 cents in paper cover, or a finer edition in cloth, for $1.75.
The Iron Mask. Being the continuation of the "Three Guardsmen," "Twenty Years After," and "Bragelonne." In one large octavo volume. Paper cover, $1.00; or in cloth, for $1.75.
Louise La Valliere; or, the Second Series of the "Iron Mask," and end of "The Three Guardsmen" series. In one large octavo volume. Paper cover, $1.00; or in cloth, for $1.75.
The Memoirs of a Physician; or, The Secret History of the Court of Louis the Fifteenth. Beautifully Illustrated. In one large octavo volume. Paper cover, $1.00; or in cloth, for $1.75.
The Queen's Necklace; or, The "Second Series of the Memoirs of a Physician." In one large octavo volume. Paper cover, price $1.00; or in one volume, cloth, for $1.75.
Six Years Later; or, Taking of the Bastile. Being the "Third Series of the Memoirs of a Physician." In one large octavo volume. Paper cover, $1.00; or in cloth, for $1.75.
Countess of Charny; or, The Fall of the French Monarchy. Being the "Fourth Series of the Memoirs of a Physician." In one large octavo volume. Paper cover, $1.00; or in cloth, for $1.75.
Andree de Taverney. Being the "Fifth Series of the Memoirs of a Physician." In one large octavo volume. Paper cover, price $1.00; or in one volume, cloth, for $1.75.
The Chevalier; or, the "Sixth Series and final conclusion of the Memoirs of a Physician Series." In one large octavo volume. Price $1.00 in paper cover; or $1.75 in cloth.
Joseph Balsamo. Dumas' greatest work, from which the play of "Joseph Balsamo" was dramatized, by his son, Alexander Dumas, Jr. Price $1.00 in paper cover, or $1.50 in cloth.
The Conscript; or, The Days of the First Napoleon. An Historical Novel. In one large duodecimo volume. Price $1.50 in paper cover; or in cloth, for $1.75.
Camille; or, The Fate of a Coquette. ("La Dame aux Camelias.") This is the only true and complete translation of "Camille," and it is from this translation that the Play of "Camille," and the Opera of "La Traviata" was adapted to the Stage. Paper cover, price $1.50; or in cloth, $1.75.
Love and Liberty; or, A Man of the People. (Rene Besson.) A Thrilling Story of the French Revolution of 1792-93. In one large duodecimo volume, paper cover, $1.50; cloth, $1.75.
The Adventures of a Marquis. Paper cover, $1.00; or in one volume, cloth, for $1.75.
The Forty-Five Guardsmen. Paper cover, $1.00; or in one volume, cloth, for $1.75.
Diana of Meridor. Paper cover, $1.00; or in one volume, cloth, for $1.75.
The Iron Hand. Price $1.00 in paper cover, or in one volume, cloth, for $1.75.
Isabel of Bavaria, Queen of France. In one large octavo volume. Price 75 cents.
Annette; or, The Lady of the Pearls. A Companion to "Camille." Price 75 cents.
The Fallen Angel. A Story of Love and Life in Paris. One large volume. Price 75 cents.
The Mohicans of Paris. In one large octavo volume. Price 75 cents.
The Horrors of Paris. In one large octavo volume. Price 75 cents.
The Man with Five Wives. In one large octavo volume. Price 75 cents.
Sketches in France. In one large octavo volume. Price 75 cents.
Felina de Chambure; or, The Female Fiend. Price 75 cents.
The Twin Lieutenants; or, The Soldier's Bride. Price 75 cents.
Madame de Chamblay. In one large octavo volume. Price 50 cents.
The Black Tulip. In one large octavo volume. Price 50 cents.
The Corsican Brothers. In one large octavo volume. Price 50 cents.
George; or, The Planter of the Isle of France. Price 50 cents.
The Count of Moret. In one large octavo volume. Price 50 cents.
The Marriage Verdict. In one large octavo volume. Price 50 cents.
Buried Alive. In one large octavo volume. Price 25 cents.

☞ *Above books are for sale by all Booksellers and News Agents, or copies of any one or more, will be sent to any one, post-paid, on remitting price to the Publishers,*

T. B. PETERSON & BROTHERS, Philadelphia, Pa.

Mrs. Southworth's Works.

EACH IS IN ONE LARGE DUODECIMO VOLUME, MOROCCO CLOTH, GILT BACK, PRICE $1.75 EACH.

All or any will be sent free of postage, everywhere, to all, on receipt of remittances.

ISHMAEL; or, IN THE DEPTHS. (Being "Self-Made; or, Out of Depths.")
SELF-RAISED; or, From the Depths. The Sequel to "Ishmael."
THE PHANTOM WEDDING; or, the Fall of the House of Flint.
THE "MOTHER-IN-LAW;" or, MARRIED IN HASTE.
THE MISSING BRIDE; or, MIRIAM, THE AVENGER.
VICTOR'S TRIUMPH. The Sequel to "A Beautiful Fiend."
A BEAUTIFUL FIEND; or, THROUGH THE FIRE.
THE LADY OF THE ISLE; or, THE ISLAND PRINCESS.
FAIR PLAY; or, BRITOMARTE, THE MAN-HATER.
HOW HE WON HER. The Sequel to "Fair Play."
THE CHANGED BRIDES; or, Winning Her Way.
THE BRIDE'S FATE. The Sequel to "The Changed Brides."
CRUEL AS THE GRAVE; or, Hallow Eve Mystery.
TRIED FOR HER LIFE. The Sequel to "Cruel as the Grave."
THE CHRISTMAS GUEST; or, The Crime and the Curse.
THE LOST HEIR OF LINLITHGOW; or, The Brothers.
A NOBLE LORD. The Sequel to "The Lost Heir of Linlithgow."
THE FAMILY DOOM; or, THE SIN OF A COUNTESS.
THE MAIDEN WIDOW. The Sequel to "The Family Doom."
THE GIPSY'S PROPHECY; or, The Bride of an Evening.
THE FORTUNE SEEKER; or, Astrea, The Bridal Day.
THE THREE BEAUTIES; or, SHANNONDALE.
FALLEN PRIDE; or, THE MOUNTAIN GIRL'S LOVE.
THE DISCARDED DAUGHTER; or, The Children of the Isle.
THE PRINCE OF DARKNESS; or, HICKORY HALL.
THE TWO SISTERS; or, Virginia and Magdalene.
THE FATAL MARRIAGE; or, ORVILLE DEVILLE.

INDIA; or, THE PEARL OF PEARL RIVER.	THE CURSE OF CLIFTON
THE WIDOW'S SON; or, LEFT ALONE.	THE WIFE'S VICTORY
THE MYSTERY OF DARK HOLLOW.	THE SPECTRE LOVER.
ALLWORTH ABBEY; or, EUDORA.	THE ARTIST'S LOVE.
THE BRIDAL EVE; or, ROSE ELMER.	THE FATAL SECRET.
VIVIA; or, THE SECRET OF POWER.	LOVE'S LABOR WON.
THE HAUNTED HOMESTEAD.	THE LOST HEIRESS.
BRIDE OF LLEWELLYN. THE DESERTED WIFE.	RETRIBUTION

☞ Mrs. Southworth's works will be found for sale by all Booksellers.
☞ Copies of any one, or more of Mrs. Southworth's works, will be sent to any place, at once, per mail, post-paid, on remitting price of ones wanted to the Publishers,

T. B. PETERSON & BROTHERS, Philadelphia, Pa.

HYDE PARK SKETCHES.

BY A. R. WESTERN.

Read the List of Life-like Sketches in it.

SKETCH I.—THE GENTLEMAN IN BLACK.
" II.—STREET-PREACHING IN LONDON.
" III.—A PARK OWNER.
" IV.—IN ROTTEN ROW.
" V.—OUT-OF-DOOR ECCENTRICS.
" VI.—THEATRICALS EXTRAORDINARY.
" VII.—A MUSEUM VISITOR.
" VIII.—THE DESERTED ROOM.
" IX.—SWELLS AND CANINES.
" X.—THE FRENCH PEOPLE.
" XI.—THE ENGLISH.
" XII.—A BATCH OF ARTISANS.
" XIII.—BENHAFIT AND A BEAR STORY.
" XIV.—ENGLAND AND AMERICA.
" XV.—CO-OPERATIVE STORES.
" XVI.—BENHAFIT IN THE PARK.
" XVII.—THE GENERAL'S FEATS.
" XVIII.—SELF-MADE MEN.
" XIX.—A TROUBLED LIFE.
" XX.—PLACES AND PEOPLE.
" XXI.—THE DRAPER'S STORY.
" XXII.—HOW AN M. P. GETS ON.
" XXIII.—GENTLEMEN OF THE BAR.
" XXIV.—VICISSITUDES OF FASHION.
" XXV.—JOHN CUFF AND THE SEAL.
" XXVI.—THE CONFIDENTIAL CLERK.
" XXVII.—THE CHEVALIER ST. GEORGE.
" XXVIII.—HYDE PARK IN SEVERAL REIGNS.
" XXIX.—VARIETIES OF POPULAR AMUSEMENTS.

☞ "*Hyde Park Sketches*" *is printed on tinted paper, price Fifty Cents in paper cover, or One Dollar in morocco cloth, black and gold, and is for sale by all Booksellers, or copies will be sent to any one, post-paid, on remitting price to the Publishers,*

T. B. PETERSON & BROTHERS,
306 Chestnut Street, Philadelphia, Pa.

HYDE PARK SKETCHES.

BY

A. R. WESTERN.

"HYDE PARK SKETCHES" will be welcomed by two classes of society; namely, by "stay-at-home travellers," and by those, less numerous, who visit the old country (as it is often called), and instead of being lost, as it were, in the immense and absorbing population of London, apply themselves to the cultivation of an intimate acquaintance with its localities and their traditions, with the inhabitants and their oft-times singular habits, customs, and eccentricities. By such a book as this the untravelled obtain instruction and entertainment from those who have visited the localities, using observation and memory together. The author has taken Hyde Park as the centre of what may be called *metropolitan* in contradistinction to *commercial* London. He used his eyes to observe, his ears to listen, his voice to inquire, his memory to retain, and his pen to record all that he had learned about the highways and bye-ways of the greatest city on earth. Original characters are described with vivid force, eccentric persons are brought forward, and the veins of fact and fiction run commingled through the pages. Nothing dull appears in these sketches, in which "the West End" of mighty London is made to pass before us, as in review. Tradition and history are blended, and a severe critic, who examined the work carefully, has expressed his admiration of the manner in which historic truth has been preserved inviolate all through. "The principal scenes," he says, "are more or less connected with Hyde Park itself, the property of the people, and the common arena upon which, *caste* being ignored for the time, all ranks, from prince to laborer, may be said to meet, as in a common centre of good fellowship. In a word, the Modern Babylon is here made to exhibit many of its numerous and various phases." It may be safely predicted that Londoners themselves, on reading this volume, will be surprised to learn how little they actually know of their own city, and how well the author is acquainted with it.

Paper Cover, 50 Cents. Morocco Cloth, Gilt and Black, $1.00.

☞ *"Hyde Park Sketches" is printed on tinted paper, and is issued in square 12mo. form, in uniform shape with "Nana," "L'Assommoir," "Hélène; a Love Episode," or, "Une Page d'Amour," "The Abbé's Temptation," "The Conquest of Plassans," "The Rougon-Macquart Family," "His Excellency Eugene Rougon," "The Markets of Paris," and other works of Emile Zola's published by us, and is for sale by all Booksellers, or copies will be sent to any one, at once, post-paid, on remitting price to the Publishers,*

T. B. PETERSON & BROTHERS,
306 Chestnut Street, Philadelphia, Pa.

www.ingramcontent.com/pod-product-compliance
Lightning Source LLC
Chambersburg PA
CBHW021842230426
43669CB00008B/1052